FEAR AND SELF-LOATHING
IN THE CITY

The Self-help Series

Professor Robert Bor (Series Editor)
Chartered Psychologist and Registered Psychotherapist
Royal Free Hospital
London

Other titles in the Self-help Series:

Fly Away Fear
Elaine Iljon Foreman and Lucas Van Gerwen

Coping Better with Chronic Fatigue Syndrome/Myalgic Encephalomyelitis
Bruce Fernie and Gabrielle Murphy

A Note about Clinical Cases in the Book

Clinical cases have been used to illustrate the tools and techniques used by the author within sessions of psychological therapy. The client-therapist relationship is based on trust and confidentiality and the author takes the privacy of his clients extremely seriously. The cases, including all names, facts and identifying markers as outlined in this book, bear no similarity to actual clinical cases with whom he has worked. The author fully respects the confidentiality of each of his clients, and any perceived resemblance to real people or events is entirely coincidental.

FEAR AND SELF-LOATHING IN THE CITY
A Guide to Keeping Sane in the Square Mile

Michael Sinclair

KARNAC

First published in 2010 by
Karnac Books Ltd
118 Finchley Road
London NW3 5HT

British Library Cataloguing in Publication Data

A C.I.P. for this book is available from the British Library

ISBN-13: 978-1-85575-652-6

Typeset by Vikatan Publishing Solutions (P) Ltd., Chennai, India

Printed in Great Britain

www.karnacbooks.com

CONTENTS

FOREWORD

The City has always attracted bright and talented people to work in its various organisations and institutions. This is what has helped to position the City of London as a hub within global financial markets. The workforce of the City is hugely diverse and people come to work here from every country. Their backgrounds are varied; some are privileged, coming from well heeled families and have received a private education; others have had to battle against the odds, coming from modest or even deprived families and communities. Both genders are almost equally reflected among the workforce; there are straight and gay people in the City; all ages are represented as are all races, religions and ethnicities.

In spite of the apparent diversity among those who work in the City, many workers share similar psychological traits and are confronted by the same challenges. Most are ambitious—even driven—, committed, enthusiastic, intelligent and may display a streak of perfectionism. A few may exhibit more questionable traits and behaviours; there are among them those who take excessive risks, who gamble, or who lead unhealthy lifestyles. Almost everyone, though, experiences significant stress from time to time, health problems, relationship difficulties (be these at home or with work colleagues), exhibit anger or aggression, experience anxieties and fears, problems with sleep, pain, alcohol or recreational drug use and of course encounter job insecurity. Some of these patterns relate to work culture as well as job and financial stresses; others stem from their personal background, peer pressure and not keeping a healthy work-life balance.

As highlighted in this book, there is still a stigma in the workplace about anxiety, depression and other mental problems. This applies even more so to alcoholism, drug use or any other behavioural signs of weakness or difficulty, particularly in the present financial climate. *Fear and Self-Loathing in the City* is a practical guide to understanding some of the psychological problems that may confront people who work in the City. It highlights ways to cope with the pressures of the workplace as well as the struggles that we have in our personal lives. It is a hugely practical book, written in a jargon-free style and which contains many case histories to illustrate some of the issues raised.

As the editor for this series of Karnac self help books, it gives me great pleasure to introduce this highly practical and insightful new title *Fear and Self-Loathing in the City*.

Dr Michael Sinclair is a City-based psychologist and has extensive experience counselling people who work in the City. This book will appeal primarily to all who work in the City and similar pressurised environments. It will also be of interest to those in Human Resources Departments and employers who require an understanding of the issues that confront City workers. It also offers practical insights into coping with the personal and psychological problems that City-based workers may confront.

Professor Robert Bor
DPhil CPsychol CSci FBPsS UKCP Reg FRAeS
Consultant Clinical, Counselling &
Health Psychologist and Family Therapist
Royal Free Hospital
London

ACKNOWLEDGEMENTS

The preparation of this book has been informed and supported by a number of different people in both my professional and personal life. I would like to acknowledge them here.

I would like to thank my colleagues at City Psychology Group (CPG) who have all shown a real interest in my work and progress, and have offered valuable advice, understanding, and assistance. In particular, I would like to thank my partner, Raoul Barducci, for his unconditional patience. Furthermore, I would like to thank Dr Hitomi Nakamura, Dr Lisa Orban, Josie Seydel, Leslie Lotz and my other psychologist and psychotherapist colleagues. Thanks also to my psychiatrist colleagues, particularly Dr Neil Brener and Dr Michael Bristow for their support through difficult times and offering experienced insight into the mental health of the Square Mile over the years. I would also like to express my sincere gratitude to Professor Robert Bor who helped to shape my academic and professional career in its early stages by acting as an inspiration, and for believing in me.

I am also grateful to my clinical supervisor, Dr Peter DuPlessis, for his continuous invaluable support, constructive feedback, and enthusiasm. He has, without doubt, nurtured my growth and confidence as a clinician over the last nine years.

A special thank you goes to the freelance writer and editor, Emma Murray, for her invaluable suggestions and advice. Thank you also to Robert Hoban for the illustrations, artwork, and book cover design.

A special heartfelt thank you goes to my family and friends, particularly: Karen Lubin, Michael Lubin, Kelly Sinclair, Andrew Johnson, Simon Meyer, and Denise G. Cox who have shown endless encouragement and carried me through difficult times over many years.

Finally, I would like to thank the many patients with whom I have been honoured to meet and work with over the years. They have offered a special gift to me by sharing a part of themselves, and it is thanks to them that I have learnt so much about myself and continue to grow as a practitioner. They made this book possible.

ABOUT THE AUTHOR

Dr Michael Sinclair
MSc PPDipCP DPsych CPsychol AFBPsS CSci MSCP

As a Chartered Psychologist with an impressive academic background and a down-to-earth nature, Michael has provided psychological therapy and coaching of the highest quality to top executives and celebrities for many years. He acts as consultant to the occupational health and human resources departments of several Blue Chip corporations in the City of London, assisting with employees' work-related stress, productivity and absenteeism. He practices from the City of London and Harley Street, and is the Founding and Clinical Director and Principle Psychologist of City Psychology Group (CPG).

Michael is an Associate Fellow of the British Psychological Society (BPS), a Practitioner Psychologist registered with the Health Professions Council, a Chartered Scientist registered with the UK Science Council, a Principle Member of the Association of Business Psychologists, a Founder Member of the Society of Coaching Psychologists, a Practitioner Member of the Register of Psychologists Specializing in Psychotherapy (BPS), and an International Member of the American Psychological Association.

Since completing his training at London Metropolitan University, the University of Essex and the Tavistock Clinic, London, Michael has gained invaluable experience over the years working in GP surgeries, specialist mental health clinics, schools, corporate organizations, and the Royal Free Hospital, London. He has lectured on a variety of psychological and other health-related topics at the Royal Free Hospital School of Medicine, Roche Pharmaceuticals, BUPA and City University, London.

Michael has published his research in academic journals and presented at international professional conferences. He is an experienced clinical supervisor and continues to be involved in the training of other counsellors, psychologists and psychotherapists.

As an advisor to the media, Michael has provided expert commentary and psychological insight on a range of topics, from breaking news incidents, to celebrity conduct. He has also contributed to many publications, including: the *Times*, the *Daily Mail*, *Psychologies Magazine*, *BBC Focus* and *Men's Health*. He has also been interviewed on television by Reuters, CNBC, BBC News, and BBC Breakfast, as well as providing live commentary on BBC Radio Five Live.

I have a friend that plays basketball—badly. Every time I go over to his house, he is in the back garden, shooting hoops with his two boys. The kids run rings around him, grabbing the ball from him at every opportunity and scoring more and more points. Although my friend is pretty easygoing it had reached a point where he was getting a bit fed up with being so thoroughly thrashed by his young children. 'Competitive dad' soon made an appearance and he began to get more and more frustrated with his inability to get the ball into the basket. Of course, this caused him to snap at his kids, as he became angrier with himself.

One time, when I went over there, he was on his own in the back garden, repeatedly throwing the ball in the direction of the basket, and missing every time. Admittedly, this was all quite amusing to watch, but after a while, I felt a bit guilty taking enjoyment in his sheer ineptitude, so I went out to talk to him.

He greeted me as I approached and then smiled, ruefully, as the ball missed the hoop entirely and bounced into next-door's garden. I thought this would be a good time to ask him a question:

'Tell me what you are thinking about when you are about to throw the ball,' I said.

'I am thinking that I better not miss this basket or I'm going to be really annoyed with myself,' he replied.

'Well, have you tried thinking about 'I can' rather than 'I can't'? And how it would feel to actually get the ball in the basket rather than how you would feel if you missed it?'

Sure enough, the next time he threw that ball it went straight into the hoop.

For me, this story really captures the essence of what this book is really about: changing the way we think. How we think has a profound effect on our emotional experience, our confidence, and consequential behaviour; if we think in a more helpful way, it is more likely that we will get the results we want.

* * *

A career in the City is an attractive proposition for many with its high-adrenalin assignments and generous pay packets, but it is certainly not for everyone. City workers in the Square Mile are put under enormous amount of pressure to perform at peak levels.

Overtime is an expected part of the deal and then there's the compulsory after-hours socializing. Many City workers find themselves torn between their work and personal lives and struggle to balance the two. They are often left feeling frustrated and anxious about their ability to manage their time and live in fear of letting people down, losing out on that bonus, or failing to progress up the career ladder.

The fact is that the City is not just a buzzing place of businesses, tall buildings, and a relentless series of meetings after meetings; it's a whole state of mind far greater than the Square Mile. The City's fast-paced working culture is contagious for some and it can encourage some pretty unhealthy habits such as boozy lunches, late nights, and skipping meals. The problem is that it's all too easy to get locked into a way of life once people start becoming dependent on the money that success brings. Some may begin to feel 'institutionalized' and wonder if they are able to cope at all without the lifestyle to which they have become accustomed.

* * *

As a City psychologist, I see a lot of people who work in the Square Mile, struggling with a whole range of emotional and mental health issues. It is quite understandable that with high-speed information technology, rising expectations, global competitiveness, loss of job security, and reducing staff levels; work-related stress amongst city workers has increased. However, most of them admit that it takes them a lot of time to realize that they are not coping very well and that they need to seek help. This is because there is such a stigma about mental health, particularly in the workplace. In such a competitive environment, emotional and mental health problems like anxiety or depression are perceived as a sign of weakness. Therefore, employees tend to hide their anxious feelings and hold them in.

However, internalising our emotional distress, generally, somatizes problems, manifesting in physical discomfort such as headache or back pain. Such is the culture of the City that most of my clients will openly admit that having back pain or headaches is far more acceptable to them than depression or anxiety.

The word 'stress' is also bandied around quite a lot in our society. 'I am stressed because I didn't make that deadline,' or 'I am ill because I have been under so much stress.' This may sound a little controversial but I don't actually believe too much in 'stress' as a valid description for how we feel a lot of the time. I think of it as a blanket term to cover underlying emotional problems that we would rather stay hidden. On many occasions, during psychological therapy, I have heard people express themselves as 'feeling stressed' when they are actually angry, depressed or anxious. As one patient put it: 'I would rather own up to feeling a bit stressed than telling everyone I suffer from depression.' Although almost one in four people in the UK suffers from depression or anxiety, there is still a massive stigma associated with these mental health conditions. Therefore, being 'stressed' is seen as far more acceptable than being 'depressed'.

Many of my patients complain about the pressures of work. In many cases, it is the work culture that demands that they work late, and avoid taking lunch breaks, or days off. It is almost that the workplace doesn't allow for human emotion. However, in spite of how we feel about our working culture, it is more about how we manage our own experience that counts. If we learn to develop a certain amount of self-awareness around our psychological states, be more assertive, and look after our own needs in a productive way, then we can deal with the pressures of the office—on our own terms.

* * *

Another aspect of the City working culture is the level of perfectionism that exists. The majority of my City patients are total perfectionists and tend to be really hard on themselves. What I try to explain to them is that perfection is an unobtainable illusion: it doesn't exist. Often, perfectionists only focus on the negatives and live in a perpetual state of fear: fear of failure and rejection. Perfectionism means thinking you're never good enough and/or never feeling satisfied with what you have achieved. Therefore, we tend to do everything possible to avoid those unpleasant feelings, for example, working 24/7, spending too much time in the gym, or drinking too much.

Perfectionists also sometimes have a habit of thinking they don't deserve success. A very common concern amongst some of the successful city workers that I have known is their tendency to feel like a 'square peg in a round hole' i.e., they truly belief they are 'fakes' and 'frauds' who don't deserve to be in such a high-powered position, and that they have only achieved so much through sheer luck and 'winging' it. Therefore, they often lie awake at night, worrying that they will be found out as useless, and that it's only a matter of time until their colleagues discover their hidden 'incompetency', and when that happens, they will be sacked!

A tough working culture can really prey on our insecurities; it is easier for an over-achiever or a perfectionist to get sucked up into the whirlpool of the working culture of the Square Mile. Insecurities like fear of failure or rejection thrive in a pressurized environment and bring out the worst in us if we allow it to. Thus, it is not about blaming the City working culture, but how we relate to it. Many of my patients have found it useful to take a look at how they can manage themselves, in relation to their own working environments, so those environments bring out the best in them, rather than the worst.

* * *

This book covers a whole range of difficult situations. Mental health problems do not just affect the sufferer but also have a great impact on those around them. Therefore, this book is not just for the person dealing with the problem but also serves as a guide to friends, work colleagues, and families to help them find the best approach in which they can support others in overcoming their problems. Sometimes we can feel helpless when we see a loved one suffer. Perhaps, the next time you see someone angry, anxious, low, upset, or drinking too much, you will be able to understand them a little better and approach them in the right way to help them deal with their issues.

Many of the chapters also deal with our relationships with others and how we can improve the way we relate to one another. If we can handle our own insecurities, become more confident, assertive and self-aware then we are in a better position to allow those around us to be themselves, and accept the way they are. By knowing ourselves in this way, we are able to have really productive and fulfilling relationships with others.

* * *

During therapy, I use a combination of four evidenced-based psychological theories, included in some form or other in this book: Cognitive Behavioural Therapy (CBT), Systemic Therapy, Person-Centered Therapy, and Psychodynamic Therapy. My patients are, by nature, rather goal-orientated creatures and so they tend to find my brief, focused and time-sensitive approach most helpful. Let's face it—with pressing deadlines and meetings to get to, we don't have hours of time to sit around in therapy. The approach and tips included in this book are collated from tried and tested hours of my therapy practice with City workers. It's all about getting productive, focusing on what works, and doing less of what doesn't work, to help move forward.

The following is my own philosophy of how those theories work, and explains the way I use them during therapy:

CBT

CBT is a widely practised method of psychological therapy these days, and it can help to bring about a quick sense of relief for those experiencing emotional and situational difficulties.

The 'C' in CBT

The theory is that if we think differently, we will, ultimately, feel differently, emotionally. Therefore, it's not just about positive thinking but about making changes in the way we think.

Others might tell us to be more positive but, sometimes, it simply isn't possible to see the positive in some situations. If we keep looking for the positive we will find ourselves getting stuck, therefore, it is unhelpful to see positive thinking behaviour as the ultimate goal we are trying to achieve. Just thinking differently, rather than positively about a situation, can bring about a profound sense of relief and change in our emotional experience. There is always another way to see a situation!

In Chapter Seven, we look at the topic of Pain Management, where sufferers experience a 'phantom' pain that, medically, doesn't exist. In this instance, a positive nature does not really help, and phrases from others like: 'There's nothing wrong with you,'; 'Pull yourself together', etc. does not encourage you to see your own situation any differently. Therefore, the cognitive or thinking part of CBT really comes in handy here as it helps us to gradually change the way we think in order to feel more at ease and confident about our situation.

The 'B' in CBT

It is almost impossible to automatically snap into a different way of thinking. Therefore, we may have to behave differently or act differently in order to think differently and, therefore, feel differently. This might involve confronting a situation that we have previously avoided or have found difficult or distressing, and making an effort to approach it in a different manner. In this way, we can try to look at the problem from a different perspective, and try to analyse the factors that cause us to feel distressed or behave in a certain way. When we confront these difficult situations again and again, armed with our new, helpful, and alternative way of thinking about them, we can learn to manage our distressing feelings in a more confident way.

In Chapter Three, we meet John, a City professional who has a drinking problem and behaves erratically as a result. His recovery involved assessing the reasons why he drank, and encouraged him to face difficult situations he had been avoiding. I also suggested ways in which he could change his behaviour. Consequently, all of these methods helped him to battle his drinking problem.

Systemic theory

Systems Theory essentially means that we are all part of a system, always connected to other people in our environments. This theory claims that there are certain patterns of behaviour or ways of relating to others around us that are the mechanisms that uphold and maintain a problem for us. Therefore, we might need to look at our own systems and the patterns of behaviour that exist between us, and others around us, to see how we can behave differently, break those unhelpful patterns of behaviour, and make changes in that system.

As an example, two people (one patient, one psychologist) in a counselling session have created a new system in the world, and developed certain ways of relating to each other; most of which are outside their conscious awareness. The psychologist will talk to the patient about their problem and suggest ways in which they can help. During this time, the patient might nod or make acknowledging sounds such as 'um' and 'ah', which the psychologist responds to and then the process becomes more circular—the more the psychologist speaks the more the patient attends, and so on. This is one pattern of behaviour that exists in the behaviour of communication between the two. If the patient stops actively listening or responding, then the psychologist may also be stopped in his tracks.

Similarly, we might experience difficult relationships with others, at home or at work. For example, you may be unhappy with the way your boss is treating you and might become frustrated as a result. However, if you look closely at the patterns of behaviour that exist between you and your boss and notice how those patterns might be maintaining this difficult relationship, then you may think about how you could behave differently to help change his behaviour towards you in a positive way.

Person-Centred theory

The main premise here is that people already have all the resources within themselves to improve their situations and deal with their emotional upset. We all have an innate tendency to be the person we want to become. However, due to expectations that are placed on us, and our innate desire to survive, succeed, and be liked in certain situations, we may adopt a way of 'being' that is out of line with who we really are, or desire to become. In therapy, patients are encouraged to explore their difficulties in a non-judgemental, understanding, and empathic forum; they are shown positive regard and acceptance.

Many people, particularly those that may want to strive forward in their City careers may find that they have to live up to certain high expectations that, at times, go against their natural tendencies to be different. A Person-Centered approach can help such people come to terms with the conflicts between what they naturally desire and what they expect of themselves, and help to change those ways of being that might be keeping them 'stuck' and in distress.

Psychodynamic theory

Psychodynamic Theory holds that another part of us is at work, known as the 'emotional self' or 'subconscious', which predicts and fuels the way we think, feel, or behave in any given situation. Chapter One explains how our emotional self may be on a single-minded mission to avoid a reoccurrence of a previous trauma, so it shuts itself off and leaves us without really knowing why we behave in a certain way.

For example, say you feel lonely and anxious about being single but then you meet someone. Initially, you are very excited and it all goes well. Then after a while, the excitement fades and despite all your attempts to impress your partner, those feelings of anxiety come back. Something blocks you but you don't know what it is; you can't seem to commit to a date and when you do, you become overwhelmed with fatigue or you find it difficult to arrive on time. Returning a text or calls becomes impossible, and then you start thinking that if they really loved you they'd try calling or texting again.

When they don't repeatedly call you, you start thinking about your partner in a really negative way, as if they're only after one thing and aren't interested in who you are. Eventually, you withdraw; they get angry and the relationship ends. Then you find you are lonely again, unsure as to why you behaved in such a way. You start regretting your decision, perhaps even thinking that that person might have been 'the one' and wonder why on earth you sabotaged the entire relationship.

Often, when we act like this in a relationship, there is a good chance that we have been 'stung' before. Perhaps, in the past, we had a relationship where we became very attached, and really opened up to the other person only for the relationship to end badly. This one experience, irrespective of how long ago it took place or whom it was with will have an impact on the rest of our relationships, often on an unconscious level. Thus, Psychodynamic Theory allows us to understand the psychological forces that are at the very source of the way we act, and helps us to, consciously, view and change our patterns of behaviour.

* * *

This book is designed to help you to overcome your emotional and mental health problems, and to learn how to provide the right support to others who might also be having difficulties. It is not to be taken as the 'experts' view nor should the reader think that the author knows what is best for them. I do not meet patients to 'fix' or take away their problems (much to their surprise!) but to join with them in a collaborative discussion so they can develop a better understanding of their situation, and implement the right changes into their lives that work best for them. I hope that this book serves as a similar function to the reader.

The case studies will provide you with a bit of background about each mental health problem, and the useful exercises and tips may help you to find a way to address your own situation. I have also used a few friendly business clichés which I have heard are quite a feature of the office language in the Square Mile (especially during 'Buzzword Bingo'!). As mentioned, I have provided the same 'quick-fix' solutions and exercises that I use with patients during my own counselling sessions, so I know, first hand, how effective they can be. So I ask you to please invest some of your time and attention and give this book your best shot!

(Please do note that the content of this book is not to be used in the diagnosis or treatment of any psychological conditions, nor is the information to be used to replace the services of a trained and qualified mental health professional.)

CHAPTER ONE

Rocking the foundations

"Criticism, like rain, should be gentle enough to nourish a man's growth without destroying his roots."

—Frank A. Clark

Do any of the following statements sound familiar?

'I'm not good enough'
'He must think I'm really boring'
'I can't believe I made that mistake; I'm such an idiot'
'I *always* say the wrong thing'
'I totally screwed up that meeting'
'That presentation I did was awful'
'I *never* make my deadlines'
'Everyone else is doing better than I am; I should be better than this'
'I just got made redundant: they must have thought I was useless'
'I didn't get promoted this year; I'm incompetent'
'Everyone got a bigger bonus than me: I'm treated so unfairly!'

1

Yes, we have a tendency to beat ourselves up. Our negative critical inner voice is always there in the background, telling us how stupid, incompetent, inadequate, and disliked we are. By setting impossibly high standards, we will attack ourselves if we don't live up to our own expectations. We also have a tendency to focus on mistakes rather than achievements and often compare ourselves with others: everyone else is more intelligent, happier, and wealthier than we are.

Because this critical voice is a part of us, and often subtly interwoven into our daily thoughts, we don't even notice it. In fact, it feels pretty normal to speak to ourselves in this way. Many of us spend our lives trying to make peace with our inner critic, without even realising it. One way of temporarily shutting it up is by satisfying our own high standards. If we achieve a goal, it can feel so fantastic that we want to strive for that feeling in everything we do. This high is addictive and reinforces the perfectionist in us. It means that when we reach one goal, we immediately raise the bar and work tirelessly to achieve the next euphoric feeling—let's face it we're emotional addicts!

Conversely, if we don't get that promotion or bonus, make that deadline or have the 'perfect' relationship, then we feel a massive low as we berate ourselves for failing to live up to our own standards.

Adopting this way of thinking often feels like we are on an emotional rollercoaster. If you think about it, the critic in us acts as a means to reach the next emotional high, it provides the downward momentum that allows us to shoot up higher with our next achievement. Without the critic, we may not get the same or an even greater buzz from our next achievement. The lower the feeling we experience as a result of our critic the higher the feeling we will experience when we inevitably succeed again.

It's got to be perfect!

The perfectionist is someone who has excessively high standards and expects to get everything just right. Aiming for 'perfection' is an endless struggle as we can always find the faults in everything if we look hard enough, whether it is giving the 'perfect' work presentation or being the 'perfect' body weight. Expecting to be perfect, and to perform 'perfectly' means that we are never satisfied with our achievements which means we will end up feeling like a failure most of the time. This can lead to strong feelings of anxiety, depression, frustration and low self-confidence.

Underneath our perfectionist ways is a strong fear of failure, rejection, and losing control. Perfectionists often fear looking vulnerable and weak in front of others. However, other people actually feel more comfortable around 'imperfect' people. It is important to recognize that is it ok to make mistakes, and that they are not a reflection of us as an 'imperfect' person. We do, in fact, learn from our mistakes, and fear of slipping up simply leaves us in a state of procrastination, lacking in confidence, and feeling stuck and inactive. It is important that, at times, we dare to be average!

Rain on your parade

Our inner critical voice has a clever way of going unnoticed. It can take many guises as it chips away at our self-confidence, intensifies low feelings, and reinforces the emotional rollercoaster of low self-worth. It can sometimes take the form of blaming others or situations around us.

Let's take Kerry, for instance. Kerry is a Management Consultant from Florida. She moved over to the UK a year ago and really can't stand living here. When I asked her why she disliked it so much, she told me that it was all because of the weather. She liked her job, her apartment, and was in a good relationship, but she just couldn't cope with the cold and rain.

Fair enough, you might think. It does get pretty miserable over here and it is always lovely and sunny in Florida, no wonder she is a bit down about it. It takes a bit of an adjustment to get over the shock of the British summer!

However, Kerry wasn't just a bit 'down'; she was getting to the point where she wanted to shut herself away from the outside world so she wouldn't have to face it:

> 'I have a ten-minute walk to the Tube every day which I dread, as I freeze or get wet. Then I get on the Tube and it is boiling and I end up sweating for the entire journey. By the time I get to work I don't even want to go in because I feel disgusting, and that I need another shower!'

Kerry was beginning to feel overwhelmed by the bad weather and had started taking time off work as she was finding it difficult to face the day. Her mood was entirely dependent on the weather and she didn't know how to handle it.

These are some of her statements:

> 'I am tired all the time'
> 'I can't cope with it'
> 'I feel useless and ridiculous for being so depressed about the weather but I can't help it'
> 'Nobody understands how I am feeling'

So, I asked Kerry to describe how she felt at that very moment when she looked out the window of my office:

Kerry: 'Well, it is gloomy and grey outside.'
  Me: 'OK, so what's the problem with that?'
Kerry: 'It makes me sad.'
  Me: 'So, what happens when you are sad?'
Kerry: 'I get tired, unproductive, and I won't feel like getting out of bed in the morning.'
  Me: 'What's the problem with that?'
Kerry: 'I won't be able to do my work and I'll eat chocolate all day and get fat.'
  Me: 'What's wrong with that?'
Kerry: 'I'll consider myself a failure because I'll get fired from my job and I will be unattractive and nobody will love me.'

So, after a bit of drilling down, I found out that Kerry was struggling with feelings of inadequacy and rejection. Once I discovered her core belief, I was able to tackle the problem at its source, and suggest practical techniques to help her get back on track.

The point is that any strong negative reaction we have towards something, no matter how simple, more often than not, comes down to the same thing: our sense of self-worth. Every time Kerry voiced her negative thoughts about the weather she was really being self-critical and, therefore, reinforcing her underlying subconscious feelings of inadequacy and rejection. In short, Kerry's negative rumination around the weather and thoughts such as 'the weather is gloomy and grey outside' ultimately equated to 'I'm inadequate

ROCKING THE FOUNDATIONS   5

and rejected!'—It seemed that she reconfirmed this to herself each time she focused on the weather in that way.

Of course, this doesn't apply to everyone who feels a bit down about the weather. These negative thoughts about the weather were Kerry's own individual experience. Only she knows her own core beliefs; my role is to help her identify them and then do something about changing them.

Our own worst enemy

> 'Man is not disturbed by events, but by the view he takes of them.'
>
> —Epictetus

Understandably, it is often the case that we become preoccupied with what might be the cause of our distress, and focus on something outside of ourselves, say our unforgiving boss, the weather etc., However, we know in psychology that it is not what's outside of us that's the problem but how we relate to, and think about, it. The environment and the events that occur around us do not 'cause' us to feel upset and distressed. It is fair to say that they do of course have an 'influence' on us but it is more to do with our own thoughts and beliefs in relation to what goes on around us that is the real cause of our distress.

Of course, most of us might have a negative automatic thought about the weather if we see that it is cold and rainy outside or about how rude and unfair our boss is if he treats us badly. However, it is ultimately down to us about how much we choose to ruminate and worry about these incidents; it is up to us how much we go over them again and again in our minds, and exacerbate our distress as a result.

The more we hold the belief and focus on how the cause of our distress lays outside of us, the more we confirm our own sense of helplessness and inadequacy around being able to change our own experience. Pointing the finger in blame to someone or something else is another way of being self-critical as it only ultimately lowers our own level of self-confidence. In doing so, we confirm that we are incompetent to help ourselves and that our happiness is dependent on someone or something else.

The following diagram illustrates how our emotional experience has nothing to do with actual events in our environment but, ultimately, much more to do with our own thoughts and beliefs about these events.

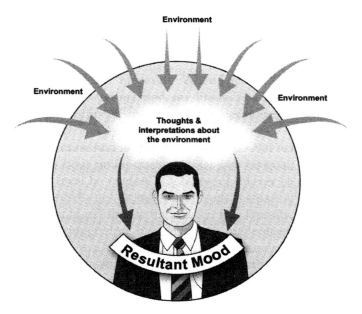

Figure 1. Thoughts and beliefs about our environment lead to our emotional experience.

It is hard not to think about negative events in a negative way and to let these negative thought patterns override our minds. When we are already low, anxious or irritated it's even harder not to think in this unhelpful way. When we are already distressed our thinking takes on a 'selective bias'. Think about it: if your boss walked past you in the office without saying a word to you, or acknowledging your presence you would be more likely to start thinking about what you might have done to upset him. If you are already feeling low or anxious, this might then cause you to worry about the implications of annoying your boss which might lead on to thoughts about the effects all this could have on your upcoming bonus. If, however, on another day, you felt more positive and happy you may think about this event in a totally different light: 'Maybe he didn't see me; he must have other things going on in his mind. I suppose that project deadline is looming … '

Why me!

Even those of us who realize that we are responsible for exacerbating our own distress often do so in a critical and, therefore, unhelpful way.

Take Raj, for instance. His eyes would well up with tears each time he spoke to me about his problems at work on the trading desk. I asked him to tell me what thoughts were going through his mind whenever he described his experience of making errors at work. As he replied, he cried some more!

> 'Well, right now I'm thinking: Why do I make mistakes? Why am I crying so much? Why can't I stop crying?'

Without even realising it, Raj was being overly self-critical about his perceived failings at work and his ability to cope with his distress.

Questions we ask starting with the word 'why' often seem loaded with accusation and judgement. By constantly asking himself 'why' questions, Raj was implying and reinforcing that there must be something fundamentally flawed with him, that he was a 'failure' and 'no good'.

Think of the last time a friend or partner asked you: 'Why did you not call me yesterday? Why haven't you done the washing up yet?' The chances are that you felt frustrated and angry in response to such critical questioning. Of course, Raj's questioning was motivated by an understandable desire to find out the cause of his distress, as if repeatedly asking the 'why' question would, in some way, reveal the 'big dark gremlin' inside him; provide the answer to his problems and alleviate his distress. However, the cause of his distress and the tears he shed in the room with me were more as a result of his self-accusatory 'why' questions, rather than anything else. Inevitably, Raj's self-questioning never gave him the answers he was looking for. Therefore, the more he questioned the more he struggled to find a solution to his problems; this led to loss of confidence and further distress.

Thus the real cause of his distress was not outside of him, nor was it buried deep within him; it was right there in the room with us. So, while Raj was in the 'now', the best way he could relieve himself from distress was to simply refocus his attention, and to try and avoid asking the 'why?' question, so often.

Shaking the foundations

By understanding the foundations of our thinking, and developing a certain amount of self-awareness around our thoughts and the impact they have on our distress, we can begin to address underlying issues that may be complicating our lives.

In psychology, there are four separate parts to the self:

- Emotional self
- Thinking self
- Behavioural self
- Physical self

These four parts are separate: we do not think in our emotional self and we do not feel emotions in our thinking self or physical self, and so on. The four parts do, however, influence one another. For example, say if you think you will not get your work presentation done in time (thinking self), you might feel anxious (emotional self), and feel your heart beating faster (physical self), and might feel the need to sit down to compose yourself (behavioural self). You may then think that taking this break is only delaying you from your work (thinking self) and you may then feel even more anxious (emotional self), and so on. The following diagram illustrates how each part of 'the self' influences the other in both directions.

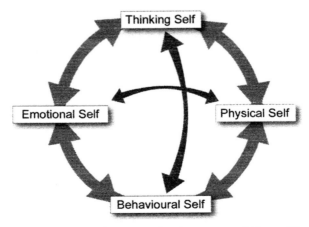

Figure 2. The interaction between the four parts of 'the self'.

The emotional self is an experience of pure emotion. It only knows desirable and undesirable emotion; the feeling it wants and the feeling it does not want. If we tell ourselves: 'I am anxious' or 'I am depressed', we are, in a way, imposing description on our emotional experience through our thinking self and language.

Furthermore, our emotional self does not distinguish between extreme environmental situational threats such as getting made redundant or being stabbed on the street; it only experiences things in black and white: good and bad consequential feeling. However, specific traumas such as getting fired or having a life-threatening experience are both threats to our self-worth, depending on how we think about them; they, therefore, threaten our survival, and, subsequently, the emotional and subconscious self may respond in a similar way to both events.

Self-worth comes down to three things: competency, adequacy, and acceptability. The majority of psychological distress is based on our perception of the levels of our self-worth in either or all of those three areas. Threats to our self-worth are also threats to our survival; therefore, it is understandable that we may experience intense emotionality in response to such threats.

Wielding the club

As far back as the caveman days, survival has been dependent on our self-worth. Of course, there were more physical threats then and with no point of reference, everything was frightening. If our ancestors weren't competent, adequate, or socially acceptable enough to fight or flee from the threat, then anything at all could end their survival.

Think about it: if you don't have the skills in place to hunt, then you won't eat; no idea how to keep warm? Well, without shelter you could die. With no interpersonal skills, you can't form relationships with others, and you would have to hunt for food and face the dangers all by yourself.

As a result, there was an innate need to be on red alert all the time, to perceive anything new as a threat; after all it was better to avoid approaching an animal that was presumed to be a man-eater rather than risk getting eaten! Keeping alert at all times meant there would be no surprises; thus cavemen lived in a state of constant vigilance, storing lots of adrenalin and physical strength in order to be prepared to fight or run away.

So, you might not think that the way we behave is similar to our caveman ancestors; after all we don't have to face scary animals today. However, the way we respond to a perceived threat to our self-worth today is exactly the same. We have learned from our ancestors that we need to think of the worst case scenario, and in catastrophic terms, in order to survive. So, say we are faced with a mountain of work emails to get through in less than an hour; we may find ourselves worrying: 'I'll never get through all these emails on time' (incompetent), 'I'll get sacked' (rejection). Subsequently, adrenalin rushes around our body which results in the physical manifestation of distress; our heart beats faster, and we are plagued by bodily aches and pains.

However, self-worth is a concept, not an emotion. Our emotional self simply has a relationship with the concept of self-worth. In fact, we have an emotional relationship with everything that we engage with in the world, including the thoughts in our minds.

There is an emotional consequence whenever we engage with any object or thought. For example, if we are really thirsty and then take a glass of water, we feel the physical quenching of thirst (physical self) but also have a desirable emotional reaction of satisfaction or relief in our emotional self.

Similarly, if we can't do something as well as others such as writing reports, for example, then we may think of ourselves as incompetent which has an emotional consequence which is undesirable. If others tease us about the low standard of the report, then we not only think of ourselves as inadequate but also as singled out, picked on and different and, therefore, rejected, which also feels emotionally terrible.

If we develop a physical illness, and are unable to walk or do things for ourselves then we perceive ourselves as being incompetent and inadequate compared to the way we were before the illness and we have an emotional undesirable feeling as a consequence of that thought.

These feelings may develop into psychological states or symptoms such as depression, anxiety, and anger. Most of us regularly use these words to describe how we feel, for example: 'I felt really depressed the other day when I didn't get that bonus' or 'I felt really anxious just before that client meeting' or 'I felt so angry when my manager told me to redo the preparation for the presentation'.

However, in psychology, we know that the words: 'depression', 'anxiety' and 'anger' are not simply descriptors for emotional experience but more for whole psychological states with distinctive emotional, thinking, physical, and behavioural parts to them. For instance, when we are depressed we feel the bleakness and emptiness in our emotional self. Our thoughts are often ones of past regret.

We may feel tired and lethargic in our physical self which may lead to changes in our behavioural self when we find ourselves sleeping a lot of the time. By contrast, when we are anxious, we feel nervous and uneasiness within our emotional self and our thoughts are often characterized by catastrophic projections, often asking 'what if' questions about the future; this can result in jitteriness and shaking in our physical self and we may (behaviourally) start to drink more alcohol, for example, to calm our nerves.

Depression, anxiety or anger can lead to disruptive sleep patterns, lack of concentration, poor memory recall, lethargy, panic attacks, poor relationship with food (and other people), problems with alcohol and drugs etc., We then perceive ourselves as not being able to function the way we used to and become depressed about being depressed or anxious about being anxious.

Mission impossible

We can understand our emotional and subconscious self as being on a single-minded mission to avoid traumatic undesirable feeling, and to prevent a recurrence of that traumatic emotional experience irrespective of any cost endured by any other part of the self. Its mission may result in conscious distress and may not make much sense to our conscious self. It is content to feel what we consciously think of as undesirable feeling because, in that way, it won't be shocked by a traumatic experience or the sudden onset of unwelcome feelings. Its goal is to avoid emotionally undesirable shocks that may occur as a consequence of unforeseen events or threats to our self-worth.

During the mission, it may employ the services of the rest of the self, including the mind (thinking self) which is where we make sense of the world and interpret the world around us. Our emotional self uses the rest of the self to look out for anything that proves us to be incompetent, inadequate, rejected etc., The emotional self wants us to experience these feelings of low self-worth immediately, before the event even materializes, so it will not come as a shock when or if it does happen.

In Chapter Two, we meet Richard, a top investment banker with a fear of public speaking. Richard thinks he is useless at speaking in public and works himself into such a state beforehand that he ends up having panic attacks before the event. In this instance, Richard's emotional self has kicked in to protect Richard from the possible emotional disaster of making a speech in public. This means that by the time Richard actually makes the speech, the worst has already happened i.e., he won't be shocked if he screws it up as he couldn't feel any worse than he already does. Therefore, it is not the actual event of speaking in public that is the real issue; his emotional self is preoccupied with 'avoiding' the shock of undesirable feeling and anxiety that may come if the event goes wrong and he ends up looking stupid in front of his peers—So, in a way, his emotional self 'avoids' that sudden trauma by bringing on the worst (emotional) feeling before it occurs by fuelling the relentless worry, and second-guessing the worst to come.

So, the emotional self is there to manage or 'avoid' traumatic undesirable feeling by second-guessing the worst. Many of us are afraid to refer to something as 'fantastic' as we feel that we are 'jinxing' ourselves, leaving ourselves vulnerable to traumatic undesirable feeling i.e., something going wrong. That means we are open to threats to our self-worth; something that our emotional self believes that we need to avoid at all costs.

As each of us has a stubborn emotional self, it is not easy for others to comfort us. It is not enough for Kerry's partner to tell her: 'Cheer up! The weather's not that bad! Get out of bed and stop over-reacting!' Nor is it helpful to say to Richard: 'What's the problem? Everybody else can manage to present in public. Pull yourself together!'

Have you ever tried to reason with a friend/partner about an issue they are struggling with? Think about the last time this happened. How did it end? Did it go well or end in an argument? Take a look at the following dialogue between a couple:

Husband: 'Jim got promoted today to Vice President of operations.'
    Wife: 'But I thought that was your job.'
Husband: 'So did I.'
    Wife: 'I'm really sorry you didn't get the job. There's always next year though!'
Husband: 'Screw next year. This is never going to happen for me. All my peers have been promoted before me; they must think I am totally useless.'

Wife: 'Don't be silly. You're being dramatic. Nobody thinks that. Stop comparing yourself to others; it's pointless!'

Husband: 'I'm not being silly. I have achieved nothing in my life. I thought our lives would get better if I got this job; what the hell are we going to do now?'

Wife: 'We'll be fine. It's not a big deal, we can cope.'

Eventually the exchange continues until one of them gets angry and walks away; the wife because she feels she is being supportive and not getting anywhere; or the husband as he doesn't feel he is being understood. The point is, no matter how comforting or supportive you think you are, nothing is going to help change those deep rooted undesirable feelings that reside in the emotional self.

Even if we are gentle with our partners and try and tell them that they are good enough, that we are proud of their achievements, and that we love them, there will always be a 'But'. In Kerry's case, her partner would tell her the weather wasn't that bad or that she might have a good day in spite of it. Yet, she would always answer: 'Yeah, *but* it's still going to be cold and I am still going to get wet if it's raining.'

Remember, the emotional self is on a single-minded mission. If it allows us to think that 'all is not bad' then it will feel less undesirable feeling but that will leave itself open to being traumatized. Nobody can fix or 'take away' our problems for us; in fact, reassurance from others just seems to exacerbate our distress at times. If you think about it, positive reassurance from others gives the emotional self more reason to fuel negative thoughts about the worst to come; there is no 'ying without yang' no 'black without white' etc. It is up to the individual to get to the heart of their own psychological experience in order to reassure themselves, and change the patterns of unhelpful thinking and unproductive behaviour that maintains their distress.

So, we know the cavemen are to blame for our innate need for survival, but in order to understand the development of own emotional self, we must look into our own past.

The monster in the closet

As children, we have all our protective tools in place at an early age. Our entire survival is based on our parents providing us with physical and emotional nourishment.

For example, say, every night when you were a toddler your parents read you a story before you went to sleep; you would be comforted by this and would sleep easy because of it. However, imagine your parents decided one night that you were too big for stories before bedtime, switched off the light and left you alone in the dark. You might lie there scared, feeling a lot of anxiety about the unexpected trauma of being left alone. Children do not have the ability to intellectualize or rationalize the experience; they haven't learned enough to know if they are competent or adequate enough to deal with the situation and they may not even have the insight to understand why they feel so anxious.

Understandably, they will tend to try to make sense of their distress and to discover the cause of it. Such an attempt may manifest itself in different ways such as imagining a monster in the closet: 'That is why I feel this way, because of the monster in the closet'; the child starts to externalize the cause of his distress. The child might sit shivering in bed, thinking about the monster in lots of different ways: does it have claws or teeth? Will it chase me around the room and do terrible things to me? The more distressed the child becomes, the more anxiety and worry they experience.

So, it stands to reason that the child's conscious self feels terrible, afraid, and anxious but, in contrast, the emotional-subconscious self feels quite comforted as it is doing everything it can to put the child on red alert should the worst happen. If the monster jumps out, the child will have all the protective tools in place to fight or run away from it; the physical self will be prepared because of the rushing adrenalin and tensed muscles; and the emotional self knows it won't get traumatized if the child is attacked as it is already prepared for the worst. In a way, the child's emotional self has latched on to and become focused on an object (monster) outside of itself to fuel this protective anxious psychological state.

If the child opened the closet and found it empty, he would feel temporary relief but, for the most part, he wouldn't dare to go near the closet, staying in bed to avoid the perceived threat.

From childhood, we tend to learn to latch on to objects in our environment in order to keep our distress or 'protective states' alive. The monster in the closet might be replaced by a fear of spiders, public speaking, making errors at work, losing our jobs, our increasing back pain, putting on weight, going insane, dying, or even the weather!

Let's take the example of the spiders. Not many of us love spiders but there are some people out there that cannot stand the sight of them. If they see a spider, they will feel anxious, run away from it, and then feel ok again. But then if they come across the same threat later on, the emotional self remembers how anxious they were the previous time and how that anxiety led to perceived safety; therefore it will kick in to heighten that anxiety once again. Therefore, we can conclude that avoiding the spider does not change our emotional relationship with it, thus fleeing from it only provides temporary relief and, furthermore, increases the likelihood of us relying on that learned coping mechanism (anxiety), again and again, whenever we encounter that creepy crawly.

Avoidance not only maintains the problem in this way but goes towards fuelling the problem over time. The more the child stays in bed the more he can worry about the monster and imagine all the terrible scenarios that may occur (being eaten up and 'rejected') if the monster jumps out of the closet. Similarly, the more we avoid that spider the more we can worry about it and confirm time and time again how we 'just can't' cope with it near us. In both examples, we are continuing to confirm the worst in relation to our incompetency, inadequacy, and unacceptability.

We also know that spiders in this country are not life threatening so thoughts that they will harm us are irrational. Every time we move away from the spider or avoid other perceived threats in our lives, then we don't give ourselves the unique opportunities to manage our emotional selves by gathering alternative evidence that we 'can cope' in that situation. We might even ask others to kill the spider for us, but that will probably still not provide much comfort. In fact, even if someone told you that they had been on a global mission to kill every spider in existence, you would probably say: 'Yeah, but are you sure one of them didn't lay eggs?'

So, the emotional self attaches itself by focusing our thinking self on to, or worrying about 'objects/situations' in our environment to ensure that it fuels our anxiety or other distressed states as long as it's doing that it confirms our feelings of low self-worth which means we can never be traumatized by unforeseen events in relation to our low self-worth.

The problem is that most of us do not know how to override this process: our intelligent self is saying: 'I know I should be more confident than this'; 'I should be able to handle this' but without the insight to address the emotional self there is nothing we can do to retrain our ways of thinking.

Thus, there is a constant conflict between the intelligent thinking self and the emotional self. Kerry knows she shouldn't be so down about the weather; in fact, she feels ridiculous for letting it dominate her life, but by not addressing the root of the problem, she will always feel distressed about the bad weather.

Second-guessing the worst

We all have a tendency to second-guess the worst by worrying unnecessarily before the situation even happens. For example, Jane worries about her partner cheating on her; she winds herself up into such a state that she is nervous and jittery all the time. This worry affects all aspects of her life, including her relationship and her job. Paradoxically, by bringing on the feelings before the event even happens, we are experiencing the same symptoms that we would be experiencing if the trauma actually occurred. Consider part of a recent conversation that I had with Jane:

Jane: 'I can't sleep and I can't concentrate at work. I keep thinking he's cheating on me. I can't stop worrying about it. He came home two hours later last night and his phone was switched off. I checked his phone when he wasn't looking. He caught me doing it!'

Me: 'I see, and what happened next?'

Jane: 'He had such a go at me! He called me crazy and said he couldn't put up with my behaviour. I just know he's going to leave me, I'm so scared.'

Me: 'It sounds like a difficult time for you. Can I ask you what your concern would be if you were not checking his phone or thinking he might not be cheating on you?'

Jane: 'Well, then I wouldn't know if he was cheating on me as I wouldn't find out.'

Me: 'I understand. And what would be the problem with that?'

Jane: 'Then one day he may just tell me and leave me!'

Me: 'That's sounds like something you want to avoid. Tell me, what would be the problem if he did tell you that one day?'

Jane: 'It would be terrible. I would feel awful. I wouldn't be able to work or anything. I wouldn't be able to cope; it would be the end of the world!'

Me: 'Tell me, how different would that experience be to the one that you're having right now?'

Jane: 'Well, yes, I suppose it wouldn't be so different. I might feel the same!'

Me: 'And with that in mind, despite it being a very unpleasant experience I'm sure, how much do you now believe that you would not be able to cope and that it would be the end of the world?'

Jane: 'Well, I suppose I could cope, somehow, in the same way I am now.'

Consider this further example, you have an appointment with the doctor and you have told your work colleagues that you need to take an hour off. However, just before you go, a work issue arises and you are pulled in to help; you warn your team that you still have that appointment but you will be as quick as you can.

So, you rush to the doctor's and it looks like you might have to wait a few minutes before he sees you. You start getting anxious: What if this takes ages? I won't be back in time to help out with the work problem. If they need me and I'm not there, that's going to look really bad. If the issue escalates it is all my fault. This could go against me when promotions are discussed. It could really affect my entire career … .

Now, bear in mind that none of this has actually happened, yet. In fact, you are called into your appointment seconds later and you end up getting back to work earlier than you expected.

The irony is that you have spent all this time experiencing the same amount of anxiety: feelings of panic, adrenalin, accelerated heartbeat etc., as you would have if the worst had actually happened; in a sense you are already living the trauma before it has even taken place.

So, if you think about it: what is the point of worrying at all? Why do we spend so many hours of our lives analysing and worrying about something that might never even happen? Are we not confident enough to know that we have the right tools in place to cope with unforeseen events and the emotional consequence of them?

Well, consciously and intellectually, yes, but emotionally and subconsciously, no. For many of us, our emotional self does not feel confident enough to manage traumatic feelings in the future. This is due to the vicious cycle fuelled by the emotional self. Although anxiety, depression, and anger are provided by the emotional self to protect us from emotional trauma in the future, such psychological states, simultaneously, go towards lowering our innate sense of self-confidence along the way.

The more we second-guess the worst by worry, for example: 'I'm going to be late', 'I can't cope with that spider' or 'I'll stammer in that presentation' the more we are criticising ourselves, lowering our self-confidence, and, therefore, increasing the likelihood that we will end up using this learned and primitive way of coping and protecting ourselves over and over again.

The following diagram illustrates the vicious cycle of how our critical thinking not only protects us from further emotional trauma but, simultaneously, lowers our self-confidence, and increases the likelihood that we use such critical thinking again to protect ourselves in the same way.

Figure 3. The vicious cycle of critical thinking and low self-confidence.

Nothing more than feelings

Our feelings are our ego; they are so significant and mean every-thing to us so it stands to reason that we need to look after them. Feelings make up a huge part of us. By trying to avoid certain feelings in the future, we are actually running away from a massive part of ourselves. By externalising the problem and latching on to perceived problematic objects and situations in our environment, we are avoiding the real underlying problems.

People often operate with a 'when' mentality: When I get this job, everything will get better; when I get married, my life will be great; when I have a baby, my relationship will mend .... However, depending on external events to make you feel better is a futile exercise.

For example, a friend of mine had an ambition to be CEO of his company. He worked every hour under the sun to achieve his goal; he would tell himself that until he made CEO, he would never be good enough. He felt that once he got promoted, he would be happy in every area of his life. He did get the job and he did feel fantastic but it was only a matter of time before his feelings of inadequacy came back to haunt him: Now I'm CEO, I need to set a good example. What if I screw it up? Why can't I ever be happy? Thus, not only was he self-critical about his own expectations he was also self-critical about his own experience.

Confronting the monster

We all need to master avoidant behaviour in order to change our experience. One of our avoidant behaviours is the way we think. If we think a certain way we learn to avoid the feeling in the future. For example, if you keep thinking to yourself that you are 'useless', you will then avoid the emotional shock of being called 'useless' or even if you suddenly think of yourself as 'useless' in the future.

Avoidant behaviour is fundamental to the fuelling and maintenance of psychological distress. It can be passive: locking ourselves in our room and not coming out; or more proactive, for example, someone with a fear of failure might work all hours and feel guilty about taking time off, because as soon as they relax, they feel they are not doing enough and have failed. Therefore, it is easier to keep busy all the time than to deal with these dreadful feelings of failure. Whether passive or proactive, avoidant behaviours are usually everyday common behaviours such as thinking a certain way, drinking, smoking, working, exercising, or eating etc. When they are avoidant these behaviours are usually either excessive or non-existent.

Only you will ultimately know what your avoidant behaviours are. Psychological therapy and this book may help you to identify them, develop self-awareness around them, and learn ways to do less of them.

However, it is worth remembering that it is not what we do but the way that we do it that counts. For example, going into a work presentation that we have been avoiding will not be a helpful experience at all if we continue to worry and notice all that we are doing wrong when we are in there!

Train the trainer

So, since early childhood, we have all been trained in different ways by our emotional self to protect us from perceived threats. Our intelligent self knows these feelings are manageable but our emotional self doesn't as it has been allowed to behave the same way over many years, and thinks it's the only way to avoid traumatic undesirable feeling and, therefore, to survive. Thus, we are dictated to by our emotional self: if I don't keep on worrying, there will be a trauma. By thinking that there is always a trauma out there, (which lowers our self-confidence) we increase the likelihood of constantly second-guessing the worst.

However, it's not that easy to try and change the way we think. This is because there is a sense of comfort in knowing that we are not good enough. For example, Matt always wanted to be in a band; he had a good voice and loved to sing. However, when he went along to an audition, his inner critic told him he wasn't good enough; who did he think he was kidding? He only ever sang in the shower anyway! Everyone would laugh at him. Believing that he couldn't do it relieved his anxiety which gave him a certain sense of comfort. He ended up leaving the audition and going home.

The point is our inner voice can really make us miss important opportunities. If we can learn to control it then we will have all the right tools in place to take advantage of every occasion and grow in self-confidence, which increases the likelihood of being less angry, anxious or depressed.

Psychological therapy helps to retrain the emotional self to understand that we can still survive and feel confident without worrying about what's around the corner. If we learn to master our thinking, we can control our negative automatic thoughts. These types of thoughts may come in the form of words/sentence structure: I am a failure etc., or a visual image, for example: you may have a flash of an image where you are being told off by your boss at work for failing to meet a deadline.

Therapy helps us to face and override our core feelings and stop living in fear. Yes, the cold weather might be depressing or I might not be the best public speaker, but I can cope with it. It is about facing our fears and realising the spider or the monster in the closet is not as scary as we first thought.

However, controlling our inner critic does not involve 'getting rid' of our self-critical thoughts. It is more about lessening them or balancing them out with less critical thoughts. So many people come to me and express their concerns about their critic. They fear if they lose their critical voice then they will develop a lack of motivation to do better or succeed. Many of these people have since discovered that it is not the excessive critical voice that helps them to succeed but, rather, a more self-accepting inner voice.

For example, consider the example of making an error at work. You could narrate this undesirable event with a self-critical voice by saying: I shouldn't have done that! I am such a loser! This style of thinking might, understandably, leave you feeling frustrated and angry with yourself. The reason for this is that you are commenting on the past event, therefore, there is no sense of forward movement. You cannot travel back in time and undo what you did. Furthermore, you are damning yourself a failure and a loser: you didn't do it the right way, so that's it, you failed, and now you are 'stuck' and unable to move forward. Such critical name-calling may not leave you with much confidence to attempt the task again, or may even leave you feeling anxious about taking on another task.

Now, consider narrating the same undesirable event this way: 'I made an error but I would like to approach the situation differently next time'. This way of thinking may not result in such an intense feeling of frustration and anger, nor will it lower your level of self-confidence in the same way. Instead, it may actually go towards boosting your self-confidence, as it suggests that you 'can' do the task again, just in a different way. It promotes a sense of forward movement as it looks into possibilities and poses the question: 'How will I do this differently next time?' You will then find yourself on the move again.

The thing is we all have an innate tendency to strive forward and act productively—to be competent and adequate is to survive. Focusing on and regretting the past goes against this natural tendency and leaves us feeling 'stuck' and under-confident. Similarly, obsessively worrying about the uncertainty of the future does the same: 'maybe I will be able do that, but maybe I won't, but then maybe I will', and so on. Focusing on what is certain, in our control and that we 'can do' in the now is in line with our natural tendency to move on with our lives, and promotes self-confidence and wellbeing.

Accepting yourself

'I feel awful! Get rid of it for me!' is a request that I often hear from patients. I tend to respond by asking them to consider what the 'it' is they want rid off. After some drilling down, it soon becomes apparent that they are, in fact, talking about their own 'feelings', their emotions—a very significant part of themselves. Of course, once they know this, they realize there is little I can do to make the feeling go away. They also become aware that they are pursuing an unobtainable goal if they think they can 'get rid' of the feeling completely.

The fact is that we cannot eradicate emotionality from our human experience. We can, however, learn ways to de-intensify undesirable feeling and to manage and cope with it in a more helpful way. Understandably, the longer we experience anxiety or depression the more we long for the opposite; we assume that our goal is to feel 'good all the time, like everyone else'. However, aiming for such an experience is unrealistic; all of us have low and 'bad' days whether we are feeling anxious or depressed, or not. It is how we think about our 'bad' days that affects their intensity and longevity.

The process of change or recovery from an anxious or depressive episode is not linear and straightforward in nature; instead it is an experience with 'up and down' times; 'good' and 'bad' days. On a bad day, if you think 'I'm back to square one! I will never feel better again', well surprise, surprise, the chances are you will feel lower for longer. Whereas, if we adopt a more accepting viewpoint around our experience and think: I feel low today which is unpleasant, but I can cope with it. I am certain it will pass again as before; we may notice that we don't feel as down about the situation. In our attempt to become less angry, low, or anxious, we would do well to lower our own expectations, and try and become more self-accepting of our emotional experience.

So, it is not about 'getting rid' of the feeling, it's about learning to become more accepting of the feeling by noticing all the things we *can* do rather than the ones we can't. By wanting to 'get rid of and run away' from our feelings (a very significant part of ourselves) we are actually reinforcing our psychological distress. In a way this fleeing process confirms an innate sense of non self-acceptance and enhances a subliminal message of self-dislike and self-rejection; it, therefore, lowers our self-confidence, making it more likely that we protect ourselves from traumatic feelings, albeit unproduc-tively, with unhelpful self-critical and negative thoughts once again. Remember it is our 'avoidant' thinking such as 'I am such a loser' that we use to 'run away' from the traumatic feeling of being a loser in the future. Therefore, if we were more accepting and less fearful of this feeling we would not feel the necessity to 'run away' from ourselves. In this sense, we would notice our negative, self-critical and distressing thoughts fade away. If we are more accepting of our distressing experiences, our feelings and symptoms of anxiety and depression will dissipate. Thus the following statements will begin to flow more naturally:

- It's ok if I make a mistake.
- Even if I get angry with my team-mate it doesn't mean I'm a bad person, but it does mean I would like to change my behaviour.
- Being a perfectionist doesn't mean I have to be perfect all the time. I am not Superman!
- The weather is pretty miserable but I can cope with it.
- I didn't get promoted this year but it doesn't mean I have failed. Success is great but it doesn't determine who I am as a person.
- I didn't know the answer to a question in that meeting but I would like to be better prepared the next time.
- I stammered a bit in that presentation but I got through it.

- Other people might put me down but I don't have to judge myself by how others perceive me.
- I was made redundant, and it doesn't feel great but there is nothing to stop me from getting another job.

The critic is everywhere; it is in the way we think; the language we use; in our behaviour and how we relate to our environment. By catching your inner critic and learning to accept yourself, you will be able to feel confident enough to deal with any situation that life throws at you.

The following chapters provide techniques, exercises and practical tips on how you can master your own negative thinking, other avoidant behaviour and retrain your emotional self. So, let's get started!

CHAPTER TWO

Under the spotlight

"According to most studies, people's number one fear is **public speaking**. Number two is death. Death is number two. Does that sound right? This means to the average person, if you go to a funeral, you're better off in the casket than doing the eulogy."

—Jerry Seinfeld

The first time I met Richard, he was shaking uncontrollably. Later, I found out that he had just had a major panic attack before coming to see me. After some time (and several gulps of water) he managed to calm himself and was able to explain the reason why he needed some help.

Richard's story

Richard was a top City banker who had developed a fear of going into meetings, presenting in front of others and partaking in conference calls. It had reached the point where he couldn't even speak in public anymore, irrespective of whether the event was social or formal.

He was a senior executive and he had never had any problems speaking in public before. Whenever he was put on the spot, he would start to blush. On these occasions, he would pass the buck to one of his colleagues and, as time went on, he would just avoid meetings altogether. Each evening and particularly on a Sunday evening, he would dread the prospect of attending meetings. He worried that he might be asked a question that he did not know the answer to and feared that he would look 'stupid' in front of his colleagues.

It all came to a head one morning when Richard was called to attend a meeting in the afternoon that he knew he could not avoid. He spent most of that morning worrying about the meeting, imagining all the possible scenarios of how it could go wrong and what would happen if he wasn't able to deliver.

As he got up from his desk, he felt the room start to spin and a sensation that the walls were closing in on him. Sweating and shaking, he felt like his heart was about to burst from his chest; he just about made it to the men's toilets where he had a severe panic attack. Following the attack, Richard left work and was signed off for three weeks. However, he still found it impossible to even consider a return to the job he had once loved.

What lies beneath

Richard's problem wasn't as 'sudden' as it sounds. Months before the attack, Richard had been feeling very anxious and nervous whenever he had been asked to contribute in meetings.

It turned out that he had been experiencing trauma in his personal life, too. His son was getting horribly bullied at school and was threatening to run away. Richard wanted to protect him but, like many teenagers, his son was uncommunicative and sulky. As a result, Richard found it impossible to get through to him, and felt powerless and out of control of the situation. Every time he tried to talk to his son, he would blush and stammer which made him feel weak and useless. In his case, this underlying sense of unease manifested itself in public speaking and brought about a range of emotional and physical symptoms, including: uneasiness, worry, breathing difficulties, rapid heartbeats, fuzzy eyesight, nausea and dizziness.

The big picture

> *'I blush—then freeze—whenever anyone asks me a question in meetings.'*

During our session, Richard told me how terrified he was that there was something seriously wrong with him. He felt that he 'should' be able to cope, and was ashamed of how 'weak' he was. Every time he blushed, he feared his colleagues would see him as incompetent, weak, and stupid. Of course, thinking this way only increased his anxiety further.

He felt that confiding in his manager or his work colleagues was too difficult, as he feared they would think him unfit to do his job. Competition is so strong in the Square Mile that this sort of attitude is very common, and many are afraid to speak up about emotional and mental health issues in case they are perceived as unfit to do the job properly.

When Richard understood that his underlying problem was 'anxiety' he felt more relieved that his feelings were real, common and 'normal' and that he wasn't going insane. However, he was still very self-critical and still felt ashamed that he actually needed help in the first place.

Barriers to entry

Richard's anxiety about speaking in public was so acute that it manifested itself in a form of social phobia. Social Phobia or Social Anxiety Disorder is a fear of making a mistake in front of others, in a way that will leave the sufferer feeling embarrassed, rejected, or open to criticism.

Of course, not many of us want to put ourselves in a position where we humiliate ourselves but, in Richard's case, he had actually developed a phobia about speaking in public. Meetings and presentations became a nightmare for him and it had got to the point where he even avoided the office canteen so he wouldn't have to engage in conversation, or eat and drink in front of his colleagues.

Relanguage

Richard had a very high level of self-criticism and frequently used negative language when thinking about his problem. He would make up absolute conclusions:

> 'I should be able to cope'
> 'I must be weak if I blush in front of others'
> 'I have to stop feeling this way'

By using this sort of rigid language and living by these fixed rules, Richard was setting himself very unrealistic expectations. When he 'failed' at what he thought he 'should' or 'must' be doing, then he perceived himself as falling short of his own expectations which resulted in low feelings, low self-confidence and disappointment.

He was tremendously worried all the time which is something that is typically characterized by lots of questions in our mind. Worry focuses on uncertainty and what's around the corner rather than what's here, right now. Worrying also tends to lead to more worry until we find ourselves caught up in an almost obsessive thinking loop of all the things that might go wrong. For example, Richard's worry sounded something like this: What if I can't answer the question? What if people know how anxious I am? What if I can't cope when I end up going back to work after my time off?

Of course, when he asked these questions he often concluded the worst, confirming a sense of 'incompetency or failure' as he saw it and, therefore, lowering his confidence further. At times, he attempted to reassure himself by rationalizing his fears but would often then question and doubt himself again. This mental and circular process of worry left him feeling even more exhausted, helpless, and lacking in confidence.

Behind closed doors

His personal life had a huge affect on his work life. At home, he believed he wasn't being a good enough father to his son and worried about his ability to protect him. He was the type of person that had a strong sense of responsibility and felt he always had to be in control at home and at work. When he thought he had 'failed' in his role as a father and protector, it impacted on his work life, too. He had a huge fear of the unknown and hated living with uncertainty (What if my son gets hurt?) and had spent his life covering all his bases so he could control the future. Thus, when the unexpected happened, he found it difficult to cope which led to acute feelings of anxiety and a loss of confidence.

Those butterflies ...

As described in Chapter One, anxiety is our natural and innate way of protecting ourselves which can be traced back to our evolutionary past. It provides us with that vital boost of energy just when we need it most to defend ourselves by flight or fight. This survival technique does not distinguish between physical and non-physical threat and, although we are not physically threatened at work, this coping mechanism is activated when we perceive other kinds of threats such as, mountains of work piling up, emails being fired at us from every direction and, in Richard's case, public speaking which all threaten our sense of survival in the workplace. If left unused, the adrenalin that gets pumped around our body when we become anxious can lead to bodily aches and pains, heart palpitations, and a whole host of other anxiety-related physical sensations.

The below diagram shows the very common physical experiences of worry and anxiety.

Figure 4. The body's physical signs of anxiety.

When we are anxious we tend to question the future and expect the worst in catastrophic terms. If we constantly expect the worst, then some part of us may feel more prepared for the worst when it happens. However, it's not the 'worst' situation we are avoiding; it's the 'worst' feeling. Second-guessing the worst to come is a way of avoiding traumatic feelings of low self-worth in the future. Of course, although we have this natural protective tendency to question; worrying proves unproductive and, as in Richard's case, only leads to more uncertainty, increases our anxiety and its physical symptoms, and leaves us feeling demoralized.

The following diagram illustrates the cycle of anxiety and how uncertainty and worrying thoughts lead to anxious feelings, anxious physical symptoms, and even more worry.

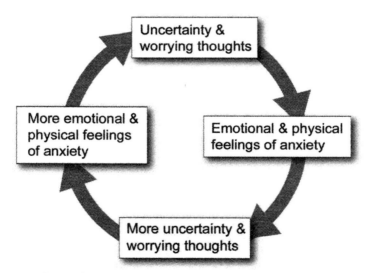

Figure 5. The cycle of anxiety.

Information touchpoint

Social phobia usually develops in childhood. As a child, Richard admitted that his parents were not very wealthy and rarely invited friends or family over to visit for fear they would be judged for their small house and inexpensive clothes; despite this, they were adamant to 'try and keep up with the Jones's'. Even going out to meet people was a big deal for them and they would spend hours choosing what to wear and where they would go. They were also reluctant to pick up the phone and make calls to others; even answering the phone was a problem.

Gradually, Richard's parents withdrew altogether, avoiding the outside world as much as possible. Thus, Richard's family life was centred around social anxiety and a constant worry about making a good impression, which had clearly had an impact on their son.

Spotting a phobia

We often roll out phrases such as 'I have a phobia about blood'; or 'I have a phobia about spiders etc.,' However, although we might say we have a phobia about something, it is generally more a dislike of blood, or spiders etc., Most of us will grumble if we are confronted with our 'phobia' but we, generally, get over it and move on. However, there are many of us that really do have a very real fear or phobia that needs to be addressed. So how do we know if we have a phobia?

The fear

Like Richard, many of us will experience intense discomfort and feelings of heightened anxiety when we are faced with our most feared object or situation. Another person would regard this fear as being completely out of proportion and excessive with respect to the actual event.

The recognition

Contrary to popular belief, people with phobias generally recognize that their fears are groundless but feel helpless to overcome them. As Richard told me: 'When I start feeling panicky when I'm in a meeting or preparing a presentation, I recognize that I am being completely over-the-top about it all, but I can't seem to stop those anxious feelings, no matter how many times I tell myself not to be so irrational.'

The evasion

Those suffering with social phobias tend to avoid public situations as much as possible, and hide away from them as often as they can. Of course, avoidance is counter-productive as they end up missing out on the enjoyment of engaging with others, and fail to give themselves the unique opportunity to see if they are able to cope in that situation. As Richard said: 'I used to look forward to meeting my colleagues for lunch and chatting about work, but now I tell them I'm too busy in case I have to chat with them in public and find I can't cope.'

Overcoming social phobia

Write it down!

Most people in working life already have a full day and feel they have 'no time' to commit to filling in a 'thought diary'. However, writing down our thoughts is an extremely effective way of gradually changing our mindset and allows for more reasoned thinking with which we can moderate and reduce our anxiety. In Richard's case, his diary went something like this:

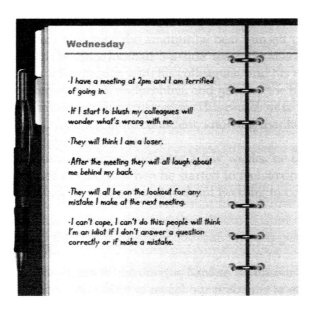

Like Richard, all of us are guilty of mind-reading others or jumping to conclusions about what others may think of us. However, this kind of thought pattern is unhelpful and only serves to chip away at our self-esteem. When I asked Richard how he would react if he saw someone blushing or stammering in a meeting, he told me he wouldn't think badly of them at all.

Often, we are convinced that others perceive us in a negative way, but this may not be the case. In fact, most people will have formed a solid opinion of us the first time they meet us and a simple instance of stammering or blushing is unlikely to change their perception of us. Furthermore, we don't tend to pay much attention to people we don't know very well and the chances of us picking up on a simple case of nerves is minimal. By negatively interpreting others, we will only ever see the negative in what they say, even though we have no facts to back up this point.

Thus, it is important to challenge our distorted thinking and offer ourselves alternatives to the way we think. So, Richard wrote down some challenges to his thoughts as below:

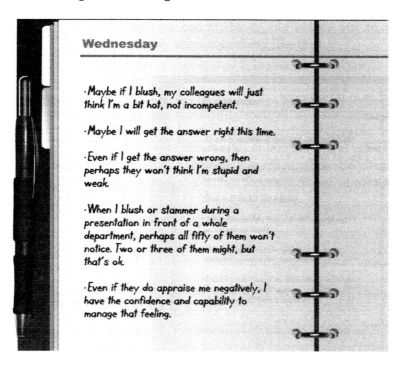

Wednesday

· Maybe if I blush, my colleagues will just think I'm a bit hot, not incompetent.

· Maybe I will get the answer right this time.

· Even if I get the answer wrong, then perhaps they won't think I'm stupid and weak.

· When I blush or stammer during a presentation in front of a whole department, perhaps all fifty of them won't notice. Two or three of them might, but that's ok.

· Even if they do appraise me negatively, I have the confidence and capability to manage that feeling.

By continually doing this over time, Richard gradually built up a mental list of helpful statements and trained his mind into a more efficient and helpful way of thinking. Writing down his thoughts also made him very conscious of the sort of language he used. When he noticed how often he used negative language like 'can't' and 'should' in his written statements, he made a conscious effort to seek alternative ways to express how he was feeling.

For example: 'I should be able to conduct a conference call', became:

> 'I would like to be able to conduct a conference call. I might not
> be able to do the call today but I will do my best to prepare for
> the next one.'

This exercise meant that Richard wasn't continually beating himself up about his fear. It also allowed him to automatically reassure himself whenever he felt unable to cope. Therefore, he was able to prevent the onset of further anxiety.

Shrinking the problem

It isn't easy to turn our worries on and off; some of us are just 'born worriers'! Richard was one of these and tended to worry all day long. Worrying or ruminating is an expression of our emotional experience; that emotional part of us is what makes us tick, and even if we try ignoring our worries, the emotional bit is not going to leave us alone—it will demand to be heard and given attention. When we try and distract ourselves from our worries, we are overriding the emotional part of us and sometimes it will come back with a vengeance if we don't give it enough airtime. Worry fuels worry but if we don't make space for it, it will end up overwhelming us.

In Richard's case, his worry was obsessive and circular; when he tried to distract himself at work from his worries, he would only end up worrying even more.

Shrinking the problem is about distraction but also giving our worries time and space. So I suggested to Richard that he allocate a specific time of the day to worrying. Here is how our conversation went:

Me: Ok Richard, so take 30 minutes at the end of the day, say,
       between 8 pm and 8.30 pm to worry. At 8 pm you start wor-
       rying and at 8.30 pm you try and worry less. So rather than
       starting and stopping the worry all the day long, you try
       and allocate specific time to it and worry less overall.

Richard: But what if I can't stop worrying during the day?

Me: If you worry throughout the day before 8 pm, try to
       write down what you are worried about and then say to
       yourself: I'm going to worry about that at 8 pm tonight.
       Then do try to start worrying about the problem at 8 pm
       that night.

Richard: But what if I forget to worry about the problem?

Me: Is that such a bad thing? Why do you need to worry in the
       first place?

Richard: Because if I don't worry things will get really bad for me.

Me: Well, how do you feel when you are worrying?

Richard: Awful, anxious, tense.

Me: So, maybe worrying less is a good thing.

The point is by worrying about not worrying, Richard actually
believed his worry was productive and it was something he needed
to do. However, over time, he noticed that when 8 pm arrived, he
couldn't actually bring himself to worry at all, and realised that worrying all the time was futile and unproductive.

   This exercise is about retraining the emotional self by telling it we
are not trying to suppress or ignore it but need some respite from it.
Giving the worry a set time each day allows us to give it the importance it deserves without impacting on the rest of the day.

   So, shrinking the problem is not about turning the worry on and
off, but about trying to do less of it. Thus, Richard persevered with this
technique and found that he wasn't worrying during the day at all,
nor was he very easily able to turn the worry on at 8 pm anymore.

The laws of distraction

So what happened after 8.30 pm when Richard's time to worry had
come to an end? Well, as we mentioned, it's not about switching
the worry off but trying to do less of it. For example, when 8.30 pm
arrived, Richard would try some gentle distraction techniques to

wind himself down from the worry. Distraction is a useful technique to retrain our mind to focus less on worry and unhelpful thinking patterns. It is important to remember that what we are trying to do here is to distract our mental activity.

Richard found that doing mental games served as a useful focus to take his mind away from worrying thoughts. He would attempt to count all odd numbers backwards from 50 in his mind. At other times he would try to remember all the names of his classmates from University that started with the letter 'S'. If he went for a walk, he would focus his attention on his environment and look out for number plates on cars, beginning with a the letter 'C', or do some people-watching, trying to guess what people did for a living or how many people he could spot wearing blue jackets etc., In social situations he attempted to distract himself by engaging in relevant activity like being the one to go to the bar to buy the drinks. He also found it helpful to focus his attention on a book, or phone a friend.

Gradual exposure

The best way to tackle social phobia is to face the fear in a very gradual way. Richard started the process by doing some relaxation, meditation, and breathing exercises (Appendices I, II, and III) each day to help lessen his anxiety about public speaking. He also used his thought diary to write down his feelings and challenge his related, distorted thinking.

The key to overcoming a phobia is to confront the fear. In Richard's case, he followed a process of graded exposure by first making a note of the situations he feared and rating them with a number from 1 to 10, relating to how much anxiety he felt in each one, where 1 equalled the least anxiety and 10 equalled the most, as shown in the next diagram.

As you can see, Richard felt better about meeting a friend for a chat but wasn't so keen to socially engage in parties or partake in meetings. Sufferers of social phobia tend to surround themselves with 'safe' friends and family and withdraw from situations that they perceive are threatening. That is the reason why Richard doesn't mind meeting his pal for a coffee and a chat as much as going along to a party; he feels safer and more secure in that environment.

Of course, it is important when facing a phobia that we start off with easier tasks rather than diving headlong into our most feared scenarios. However, in order to really challenge a phobia, we do have to, gradually, step out of our comfort zone and set achievable goals towards confronting a threatening situation and feeling.

Fight or flight

When Richard eventually went to a party, he started to feel anxious and panicky. His first instinct was to run away from the situation. However, the more we avoid situations the worse they will be when we return to them. If we learn to stay in the moment, we will, at first, feel heightened symptoms of anxiety. However, the intensity of these feelings will dissipate each time we put ourselves into the feared situation; they may not be pleasant but they are not life-threatening and they will go away. It is not the end of the world if we have intense anxious feelings. Knowing that they will decrease is the first step towards conquering a phobia.

The following diagram illustrates how our anxiety levels lessen each time we confront our fears and shows how we become less avoidant of situations over time.

Thus Richard learned to stay in the situation even when he wanted to take flight from it. He also used breathing and distraction techniques and helpful self-talk coping statements to quell his

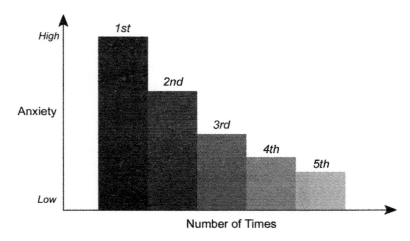

Figure 6. Anxiety decreases each time feared situations are faced.

feelings of panic and anxiety. This helped him to understand that he could get through an unpleasant experience which gave him the confidence to face that experience again and again until he didn't feel anxious about it anymore.

During his time off work, Richard very gradually became more involved in more social activities. He would have a coffee with a good friend of his or attend a school event with one of his kids. The more social engagements he went to the more confident he became about having a conversation in public without stammering or blushing. After a couple of weeks, Richard began to think about a return to work.

Critical path

When Richard 'screwed up' in a meeting he would immediately focus on the negative:

> 'I was terrible in that meeting. Everybody could see what state I was in. I stammered and blushed and couldn't answer a couple of questions.'

When I asked him if he could tell me what was good about the meeting, it took him a long time to respond. He told me, rather reluctantly, that he had actually come up with a few ideas in the meeting that his colleagues seemed to really like. On further investigation, he also admitted that he had answered other questions correctly. By the end of our discussion, he was able to see the situation hadn't been as bad as he had first perceived it. This made him feel better about how he had behaved in the meeting and gave him the confidence to eventually attend another one without feeling so fearful of it.

So, no matter how bad a situation appears to be, it is always important to look for alternative viewpoints to it. When we do, we come to realize that, perhaps, our 'terrible' experience was not as bad as we first thought.

For example, say, like Richard, you have a fear of public speaking but you stand at the top of that room and deliver the presentation anyway. You might stammer and shake all the way through it and feel awful afterwards, but it is important that you give yourself credit for getting up there and facing your fear in the first place, rather than running away from it. If you continually do this and look for alternative ways to see the worst-seeming situations then you will find you won't feel as nervous and anxious the next time you have to do a presentation.

Thus, acknowledging and praising our achievements, no matter how small or unimportant we think they are is also fundamental in rebuilding our confidence. It is important to come up with self-praising statements and repeat them to yourself over and over again, even if you do not believe them at first! The more you repeat them the more you will believe them and feel the genuine desirable feeling when you say them. It is only because Richard relentlessly repeated to himself that he 'looked stupid' in front of his peers, that he came to feel this as genuine, and perceived it as his actual reality.

Do's and Don'ts for conquering a phobia

- *Don't* rush headlong into facing your phobia. This might overwhelm you and reinforce the feelings of panic and anxiety.
- *Do* take small steps towards addressing your phobia. Set yourself achievable goals. Remember, if you keep on avoiding the situation, you might never get over your phobia.

- *Don't* hide yourself away. Take up a hobby or a sport that involves engaging with others. This will help to build up your confidence which will have a positive effect on other areas of your life.
- *Do* challenge your negative thoughts by writing them down.
- *Don't* constantly focus on your phobia. Try and shift your focus by imagining scenarios where you are really enjoying a social event. Imagine how it feels to be full of confidence and being able to have a great conversation with a group of people.
- *Do* make lists of positive appraisals about yourself and repeat them time and time again.
- *Don't* catastrophize when you are confronted with your phobia. Use positive statements to reassure yourself that you are not in any real danger, and that you have the power to choose how you react to the situation.
- *Do* practice distraction, breathing, meditation, and relaxation techniques to help you manage your anxiety and fear. These will help to keep your mind and body calm and relaxed.
- *Don't* ignore your phobia. Make an effort to understand what it means to have a phobia and learn as much as you can about the process for overcoming your condition.

Back in business

Richard made a gradual return to work but was excused from attending any meetings. This was a crucial part of his recovery as he no longer felt under pressure to perform in group discussions. It also gave him time to imagine scenarios of how the meetings would be when he returned and allowed him the option to choose which meetings he would eventually attend. This gradual approach put him in control of his own environment and helped build up his confidence.

In due course, he felt comfortable enough to go to meetings and, in time, began to contribute to the discussions without feeling embarrassed or afraid. He also felt strong enough to confide in his work colleagues about his problem and was amazed at how supportive and understanding they were. When speaking to them he was also pleased to discover that they also experienced similar feelings in meetings.

Richard also came to realize the futility of worry and the destructive affects it had on his anxiety levels and self-confidence. He did come up with answers to his questions which he found more accept-able. Also, he learned that if he didn't have the answer to his col-leagues' questions or if he blushed in meetings then it wouldn't be the end of the world—he started to feel he could cope with these potential undesirable events. He also came to accept that in life, there is always a certain degree of uncertainty; in doing so, he felt more at ease with his experience than when he constantly tried to be certain about every outcome.

Ultimately, Richard learned not to be so preoccupied with how others perceived him and learned to be more accepting of his own thoughts and feelings.

Sea of uncertainty

Trying to eradicate uncertainty from our existence is simply not going to happen. We may not feel comfortable with the prospect of uncertainty and might be fearful of what lurks just around the corner, spending all our efforts trying to cover all our bases and second-guessing the worst to come. The truth is the more we try to seek certainty, the more anxious and fearful we will become. The fact is that uncertainty is a part of everyday life; it is something we cope with on most days, sometimes without even realizing it. Think about driving along a dark country road at night. Sure, your head-lights light up the road in front of you, but there is only so far into the distance that you can see. Somehow, however, we trust and have some confidence in the fact that the road will go on, and the next part of the road will just fall into place in front of us, as we approach it.

Life is kind of like that. We would do well to try and remain con-fident about our ability to manage whatever experience we have in the future when we get there. Remember, it's our self-critical think-ing and worry around what is uncertain that leads to a lack of self-confidence, and a feeling that we may not cope in the future. So if we try and fear uncertainty less, and worry less, we may feel more confident that we *can* cope with whatever life has to throw at us!

Touching base

Richard began to address his relationship with his son by first writ-ing down and challenging his fears. He also imagined what it would be like to have a really good conversation with his son and how it would feel to be able to successfully fix the problem. Therefore, when he approached his son he was already in a state of confidence and reassurance.

By adjusting his language and mindset, Richard felt strong enough to engage with his son. Rather than blaming his son for being sulky and uncommunicative, he expressed his concerns in an assertive, honest way. (Please see Chapter Eight for some more tips on how to communicate effectively with others.)

In turn, his son was more empathic and responsive and they were able to have a productive conversation.

The upshot

Anxiety underlies and fuels the discomfort we feel when we are 'put under the spotlight'. The corporate world is highly competitive and therefore when 'all eyes are on us' as an individual it is understandable that we have fears of not delivering and surviving in this demanding and cut throat environment.

Uncertainty is something that we all need to learn to live with. It is only when we try to run from it that we become more fearful of it. By challenging our thoughts, gradually approaching feared situations again, and using techniques such as distraction, breathing, meditation, and relaxation etc., we can grow in confidence and learn to overcome our intensifying fears.

Anxiety is a very real problem that affects most of us at one stage or another. It manifests itself in a number of ways including panic attacks and phobias. Once we address the underlying feeling of anxiety we will find that our fears dissipate over time.

CHAPTER THREE

Power cut

"When you stop drinking, you have to deal with this marvellous personality that started you drinking in the first place."

—Jimmy Breslin

Work is such a fundamental part of our lives. Given that most of us spend more time at work than anywhere else, it is not surprising that it plays such an important role. Work gives us a sense of forward movement and productivity which is essential to our sense of self-worth and therefore, survival. It can give us a boost to our self-esteem and helps us relate to different types of people. However, a poor working environment can trigger more negative feelings and responses which not only affect work but our personal lives too. Sometimes we bury ourselves in work to avoid these unpleasant feelings. When we do that, it's only a matter of time until we 'blow up' or burn out.

John's story

When John first came to me, he was drunk. It doesn't take a psychologist to know when someone has had a few drinks, but John's state of inebriation was particularly memorable. He practically fell into my office and then, red-faced, began to crack jokes for a good few minutes. I knew he was just trying to distract me from beginning the session, but he was truly hilarious. It took a bit of time for both of us to gather our composure, but once we had calmed ourselves, we began to talk.

It didn't come as a major surprise that John had a drinking problem. It was great that he had found the courage to come and see me but, at the time, he really didn't have any intention of stopping what he was doing.

He was a slightly overweight man in his late 40s; a top executive in the City, highly intelligent and a total perfectionist. Following an office restructure, he had been moved from his own private office (for which he had fought long and hard) to an open-plan environment. As a result, he began to feel stressed at the level of noise and was constantly distracted by the people 'dropping by' his desk.

Prior to the move, John had enjoyed a quiet working life in the confines of his own office and couldn't cope with the new environment. He began feeling very low, taking it personally when people chatted around him, and felt like they didn't respect him enough to keep the noise down. He also found it difficult to say no to those who kept piling more stuff on his desk for fear they would think he was incompetent.

As he became more and more depressed, he started to drink heavily during the day. Entertaining clients was a large part of his job and often work meetings turned into boozy lunches. However, when he was feeling down and under pressure, he found himself drinking over two bottles of wine at these client lunches.

As his work volume increased, he began feeling more and more out of control. He would go to work in the mornings, feel stressed out after a couple of hours, leave work in the early afternoon, and go to bars and strip clubs for the rest of the day. He reasoned that he wouldn't be of any use at work after a few drinks anyway, and was also afraid that if he returned, his work colleagues would suspect how drunk he was.

As time went on, his behaviour became more and more erratic. If people popped by his desk, he would feel more agitated and struggled to form the right words through lack of concentration. Instead, he would have aggressive outbursts which led to a breakdown in his working relationships. He felt people hated him as a result and became quite introverted and isolated at work. Of course, all this made him feel even worse about himself so he would hit the drink to numb those undesirable feelings.

While he was at the bars and strip clubs, he would spend a huge amount of money on wine and expensive cigars; money he didn't even have. He would then feel guilty about what he was doing, and drink some more to quell the disgust he felt for himself.

After a few months of this erratic behaviour, John walked out of work and never went back that day. Too ashamed to admit to his family or work colleagues what was going on, he took a few days sick leave to try and get himself together.

Escalation

John also had a wife and a couple of children. He had been married for over 15 years but somewhere along the way, he felt he had lost the ability to communicate with his wife. They began to drift apart and he felt rejected in the bedroom. He also drank at home during the evenings and weekends to numb the uncomfortable feelings around his wife. Needless to say, his wife knew nothing about his excessive drinking, his visits to strip clubs or any of the pressure he was under.

He also had other problems going on in his personal life; his mother had died quite recently. She was a highly critical person who he had fallen out with on many an occasion. John never got a chance to repair their relationship before she died; something which he deeply regretted and now felt was out of his control.

Power trip

It was clear that John had lost all his confidence. With few satisfying endeavours and relationships outside work, he had completely relied on work to validate his self-worth; his self-esteem was entirely dependent on his job. When he was 'demoted' from his office to an open-plan area, he felt disempowered and, in a sense, emasculated. Suddenly, he felt that people didn't respect him anymore and he lost confidence in his ability to carry out his job.

By spending large quantities of money on drink and strippers he also felt manlier, more powerful, and in control. It made him feel important. After a few drinks, he also felt he was able to think creatively and would feverishly jot down lots of ideas, which made no sense to him after he had sobered up. However, he felt he could only think with some element of fluidity when he had been drinking, and so continued with the illusion.

The demon drink

Although John was concerned about his drinking, he felt he would be unable to give it up as it was a major part of his working life. When entertaining clients, the expectation was to have a meeting over a few bottles of wine; in fact, it was an important bonding process. He felt that if he stopped drinking, he wouldn't be able to engage properly with his clients and the relationships he had with them would fall apart.

Although it affected his productivity, alcohol gave him a false sense of confidence, but only for a short period of time. When he sobered up, he would beat himself up about his drinking, feel low, and then start drinking again to numb his feelings of low self-worth.

His angry outbursts gave him similar short-term relief. By being aggressive, he felt bigger and more powerful in front of his work colleagues. However, he would then regret his actions, chastise himself severely and feel low as a result.

Zero sum game

The language we use is very important as it influences how we feel emotionally and the way we react to our circumstances. In John's case, he would repeatedly beat himself up and criticize himself:

> 'What I am doing is wrong. I am a terrible person. I am a complete failure, a total loser . . .'

Like many high-achievers, John was a total perfectionist. Typically, perfectionists are people with excessively high standards who have to get everything just right and constantly strive for more and more. They are driven by a fear of failure and rejection and do everything they can to avoid these feelings. This might mean spending excessive time at work, too many hours in the gym, checking work time and time again, drinking too much in social situations, or not showing vulnerabilities to others.

These 'avoidant' behaviours are understandably a quick fix; they prove unproductive in the longer term and lead to more distress and feelings of failure. Gradually, John realized that perfection was an unobtainable illusion and he knew he would have to face his fears in order to move on with his life.

Crossing the chasm

As a first step, John found it very useful to keep a 'self-monitoring drinking diary'. He found it gave him a clearer picture around the severity of his drinking. Also, by entering the incidents of drinking into his diary, it encouraged him to think twice before having another drink. John kept a record of when, where, and with whom, he drank and how many units he drank each time. This is how his self-monitoring diary looked after the first week:

Day	Morning/Units	Afternoon/Units	Evening/Units	Total*
Mon		At strip bar alone / 4	At strip bar with strippers / 6	10
Tues			At home watching TV, wife in the other room/ 3	3
Wed		At work lunch with clients / 6	At bar alone / 6	12
Thurs	At bar / 3		At home / 6	9
Fri		At work lunch with clients / 8	At strip bar with strippers / 10	18
Sat			At home watching TV alone / 3	3
Sun			At home alone / 4	4
			Week Total	49

*One standard unit of alcohol = one half-pint of average beer/lager; one glass of wine, one standard single measure of spirit. Recommended cut off number of units: men = 28; women = 21 per week.

Doing your homework

One of John's main problems was feeling out of control of himself and his environment. Along with a self-monitoring diary, writing down our thoughts is the next step towards achieving some control and gaining a new perspective on our situation. In doing so, we start to realize how our thinking influences our feeling and that we are, in fact, able to be in control of our emotional experience and behaviour. When John returned to work after a few days, he began to write down his thoughts and related feelings when he was in the office, like below:

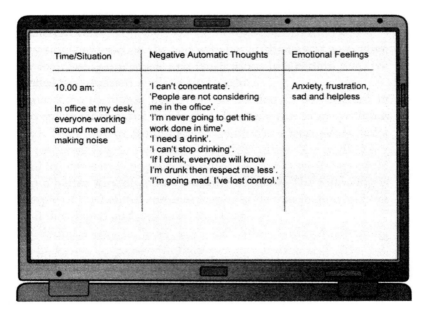

Time/Situation	Negative Automatic Thoughts	Emotional Feelings
10.00 am: In office at my desk, everyone working around me and making noise	'I can't concentrate'. 'People are not considering me in the office'. 'I'm never going to get this work done in time'. 'I need a drink'. 'I can't stop drinking'. 'If I drink, everyone will know I'm drunk then respect me less'. 'I'm going mad. I've lost control.'	Anxiety, frustration, sad and helpless

By reading through his thought diary, John realized that his relentless and negative automatic style of thinking was the reason for his intensifying negative feelings.

The big challenge

The trick is to challenge our automatic negative thinking. For example, 'I can't' could be changed to 'I'm just not able to do it right now the way I would like to . . . ' This leaves the situation more open-ended rather than forcing us into corner, and makes us feel more hopeful and accepting of our experiences; alleviating some of our distress. We can use similar methods to keep our anxiety at bay:

> What if I don't get this work in on time?
> What if people think I'm incompetent?
> What if I lose my job?

By challenging these worrying questions, we can come up with less catastrophic answers, helping us to manage our anxieties a bit better.

John challenged his thoughts about what he perceived others thought about him. For example, perhaps people wouldn't mind if he missed the deadline and not see him as a loser as a result. He also realized that maybe he could cope with the feeling around missing a deadline and what others thought of him.

Over time, he began to understand the futility of worry and rumination and becoming preoccupied with what he 'should' and 'shouldn't' be doing.

The futility of shoulds

'I should' is an absolute statement and a dangerous one as it only reminds us of our own shortcomings. The words 'I should not' in the statement 'I should not drink' for example, allow no possibility for flaw or failure and when the inevitable drink happens we might conclude that we are entirely hopeless and a failure: all on the basis of a single drink!

John felt he 'should' be functioning and coping 'normally' and felt like a failure because he wasn't managing the way he 'should' be. We often use explicit statements like 'I am stupid', 'I'm an idiot' etc. which are destructive to our self-worth and self-esteem.

Although using the word 'should' is less explicit than harsh statements, it is actually more damaging, as the more we use it, the more it monopolizes our thoughts, all the time going unnoticed and affecting our self–confidence. For example: 'This shouldn't have happened', 'I shouldn't be here', 'I should be doing something else'. This constant mental scolding that is subtly interwoven into the way we narrate our experiences, makes us feel like we have failed in life, and it devastates our confidence.

If our confidence and self-worth decrease, then we turn to other pursuits (excessive drinking, working 24/7) which give us a false sense of self-worth and coping, and mask our insecurities and vulnerability.

The big 'D'

Negative thoughts and language that focus on the past and the present can be a sign of depressive behaviour. 'I should have done this' or 'I can't do that' are statements that imply that there is no way out. When we realize we can't change what's happened in the past it renders us helpless, powerless, and stuck and leaves us feeling even more under-confident.

In contrast, the worry associated with anxiety is based on the future usually signified by 'What if?' questions and other catastrophic projections. Again, we can't control the future so it is best to focus on the present and figure out what we can do right now to get ourselves moving forward again.

The drinking chronicles

John couldn't figure out how he ended up leaving his desk to go to the pub or a strip club during the day, and not returning to the office. Like the thought diary, John started on a diary that charted his drinking habit. He made a contract to himself to do something to address his drinking and to write down his drinking habits and all the reasons why he drank to such an extent.

He began to break down his journey from the office to the pub to the strip club and wrote down where he was and what he was thinking and feeling at the time. His first diary entries can be seen in the following extracts.

As the diary entries continued, John began to realize how damaging his thinking and other behaviour was to himself. He noticed that he was stuck in a vicious cycle and that his drinking was a way to avoid the uncomfortable feelings associated with his work situation and his drinking behaviour itself.

Reporting before the drinking behaviour:

Time/Situation	Negative Automatic Thoughts	Emotional Feelings
11.00 am: I'm sitting at my desk and people keep bothering me with extra work and questions.	'I can't concentrate'. 'I have to get out of here.' 'I'll have a drink later'	Frustration and anxiety. Secure, content, excited

Reporting during the drinking behaviour:

Time/Situation	Negative Automatic Thoughts	Emotional Feelings
3.00 pm: In the bar drinking on my own.	'I won't be able to meet my deadline in work'. 'I can't return to work because I have had too much to drink and people will know that I'm a drunk'. 'I can't stop drinking.'	Anxious and sad
4.00pm: Still in bar. Strippers have started dancing.	'I'll have another drink and a cigar, that will help' 'I think that stripper is looking right at me!'	Secure, in control, content, excited

Reporting after the drinking behaviour:

Time/Situation	Negative Automatic Thoughts	Emotional Feelings
7.00 am: Next day on the train on the way to work.	'I drank three very expensive bottles of wine by myself and spent over £200 on private dances from strippers'. 'I hate myself for being so stupid and so weak.' 'I can't cope' 'I need a drink!'	Sad, helpless, out of control.

John also began to make lists about how his drinking was affecting himself and others. From these lists, he realized that his excessive drinking was having a negative impact on his relationships at work and at home, as well as his health. By recognizing the negative associations with alcohol he was able to take steps to address his behaviour and change his lifestyle.

The following diagram shows how we can get caught up into a habit of drinking when we rely on it to manage our negative thoughts and feelings while it continues to affect our lives in a problematic way.

Writing diaries about our thoughts, feelings and behaviours is a helpful intervention that we can apply to ourselves. With most habits, we are driven by our emotions and subconscious. Most of us consciously know that smoking and excessive drinking is bad but we can't seem to stop. Intervention techniques, such as writing things down, are a way of making our subconscious more conscious and gradually help us to gain control over our emotions and break the pattern of habitual behaviour.

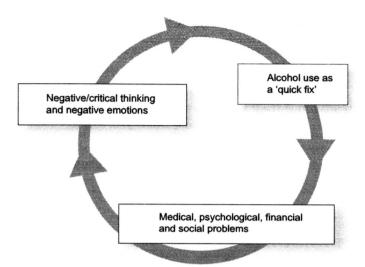

Figure 7. The vicious cycle of problem drinking.

Thinking outside the bottle

As John continued with his diaries, he became aware of the patterns of his behaviour and the link between his drinking and his underlying sense of self-confidence. He began to realize that he could boost his confidence in other more effective and long-lasting ways. Therefore, he worked hard to reduce the amount he beat himself up by joining the gym, and the office football '5-a-side' team. He also made time to work on his relationships with his colleagues, and his wife.

As we know, exercise builds endorphins, and releases the bodily tension built up from anxiety and frustration. This causes us to feel a lot better, physically. John felt more confident, knowing that he was losing weight and improving his fitness.

His thought patterns changed and after a few weeks, he didn't even need the diaries anymore. When he started to feel anxious or low he was able to talk himself out of it without needing to consult the diaries.

Spreading the news

Breaking a habit like excessive drinking is hard to do on our own. Although it may seem impossible to reveal our problems to others, it is so important that we let them know what has been going on. This way, they are in a better position to help and support us when we are trying to overcome the problem.

For example, John made a promise to himself that he would try and cut down on his drinking. He told his wife his intentions and asked her to help him get through those difficult moments whenever he felt tempted to have a drink. When he started to communicate with his wife about how he was feeling, he was surprised and gratified at her understanding and supportive reaction.

He realized that, with her support, he no longer needed to drink excessively, or go to strip clubs to feel more empowered. They grew closer and started to spend more time together, which made him feel more in control of his own environment.

The following are the rules he made for himself:

- I will try not to drink in the morning.
- I will try to only drink at lunchtime when I am entertaining clients.
- If I drink, I will try to drink no more than two glasses of wine.
- I will try not to drink spirits.
- I will try not to drink at the weekends.

The next time John felt a craving for alcohol, he was able to tell his wife, and she talked him through it until he felt better again. Through their conversations, he was able to see that he didn't 'need' a drink; he only wanted one because he felt anxious and was relying on the alcohol to avoid those unpleasant feelings.

His wife also helped to distract him from his cravings. She would suggest that they go for a walk or go to the cinema; and encouraged him to engage in other activities that didn't involve drinking such as going to the gym, or playing football with his work colleagues.

The point is that without the support of others, breaking a habit becomes an intense struggle, and is more likely to end in failure.

Rules are made to be broken

There is debate as to whether total abstinence or 'controlled reduced drinking' is the best way forward to stop our drinking habit. Some may, of course, find abstinence an easier way to achieve their goals.

It may be harder for some to stop themselves from binging on alcohol, especially when they have already had one or two; so, in that situation, wiping out all drink may indeed be the best way to go. However, some of us often set unrealistic rules for ourselves when we are trying to kick a habit. Going 'cold turkey' often puts severe pressure on us and can set us up for a fall. If we say 'no more drinking' and we do have another drink, it can make us feel worse and we are more likely to quickly return to our old habits as a result.

It is important to realize that we are all human, and making mistakes or having occasional relapses is a perfectly normal part of our makeup. Although we might feel devastated when we fail, the most important thing is not to 'beat ourselves up' and not to give up. The world is not going to come to an end if we make a mistake, and it doesn't mean we cannot achieve our goals. See it for what it is: a hiccup; and then try again.

It is maybe more realistic to set manageable goals. For example, as we have seen, John made the decision to try and not drink at weekends. He felt it would be impossible not to drink during the week as drinking and entertaining his clients was a large part of his job.

The first weekend arrived and John got drunk. Instead of beating himself up about it, he entered it into his drinking diary:

Thoughts: I have drunk two bottles of wine this weekend. I would like to try and drink less next weekend.

Feelings: Slight disappointment but hopeful

The less hard we are on ourselves, the less inclined we are to keep up the habit. If John drinks again the following weekend, he can also enter that into his diary, all the time writing down how he feels after drinking and the way he thinks about it:

'Next time, I will have two glasses of wine rather than two bottles because I know that after the second bottle I get tipsy and depressed.'

For a perfectionist like John, this was a method that suited him. He learned, over time, that rules aren't rigid. It wasn't the end of the world if he didn't meet all his targets. As he began to reach his drinking goals, he felt more in control and empowered. The more confident he became, the less he drank.

Pat on the back

It is also important to reward ourselves for achieving our goals. When John made it through the following weekend without having a drink, he treated himself to a gadget he had had his eye on for a long time. Rewarding ourselves for our achievements, no matter how small we think they are, is important in order to motivate us along the way. Rewards remind us of all our efforts and what we have achieved and, therefore, go towards boosting our self-confidence. Remember: an underlying sense of self-confidence enables us to feel that we don't need to turn to that drink each time we feel overwhelmed.

Craving your goals

Once we have reduced the amount we drink, we may still be haunted by cravings for another drink, especially when we are in stressful situations. It is important to keep a mental checklist of helpful tips to help you beat those cravings when they come. John kept a list of these on his laptop as you can see below:

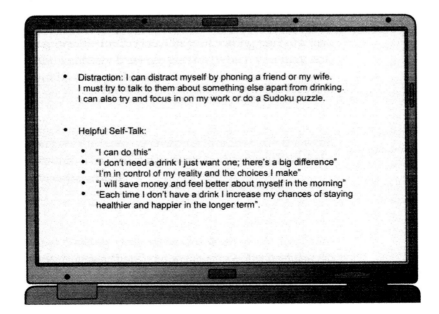

- Distraction: I can distract myself by phoning a friend or my wife. I must try to talk to them about something else apart from drinking. I can also try and focus in on my work or do a Sudoku puzzle.

- Helpful Self-Talk:
  - "I can do this"
  - "I don't need a drink I just want one; there's a big difference"
  - "I'm in control of my reality and the choices I make"
  - "I will save money and feel better about myself in the morning"
  - "Each time I don't have a drink I increase my chances of staying healthier and happier in the longer term".

Back to work

John's newly returned confidence gave him the courage to address issues at work. If his colleagues piled work on his desk, he operated a 'rain check' system, which made him feel assertive rather than aggressive. By doing this, he also gained a sense of empowerment over his ability to manage his relationships.

He, bravely, expressed his limitations to his colleagues and was pleasantly surprised by their understanding responses. He began to trust in his colleagues' abilities more and delegated work to them, something that he had feared doing before. (Please refer to Chapter Four for more information and tips about delegation).

Furthermore, John deliberately attempted to lower his excessive standards when carrying out tasks and limited the time he gave to tasks. He realized that doing what he could, in the time available, did not lead to the end of the world, and business simply continued. He made an effort to savour the moment and tried not to worry about the outcome all the time which allowed him to enjoy his work more.

Tips for beating the demon drink

- Write down your reasons for cutting down the drink.
- Make a written contract setting out your intention to cut down.
- Write out rules and set achievable goals to carry out these rules.
- Remove all temptation from your environment by locking away or getting rid of the alcohol.
- Self-monitor your drinking to gain more awareness and control around your habit.
- Use a 'Drinking Chronicles' diary to establish your thought, emotional and behavioural patterns.
- Commit to making some lifestyle changes.
- Drink slowly and pace yourself.
- Distract yourself by doing something enjoyable and healthy, like going for a walk or playing sports.
- Ask for help and support from family, friends, work colleagues or a therapist.
- Try not to drink when you are feeling depressed or anxious. This will only exacerbate the situation.

- Try and stay away from places that make you feel like drinking, like clubs, pubs etc.
- Avoid drinking with other heavy drinkers as this will only encourage you to drink even more.
- Make a list of helpful tips to beat those cravings.
- Expect an occasional relapse but, most importantly, try not to give up!

Breaking the spell

It took two months for John to change his mindset and grow in confidence. He became less critical and more accepting of himself and developed better relationships at home and at work. Through therapy, he was also able to address the feelings of guilt he had about his relationship with his mother, and, finally, came to terms with her death. John never quit drinking altogether but he learned to moderate it and now feels he has it under control.

Lead, follow or get out of the way

John's behaviour could be classified as 'Type A'. He was a total perfectionist with an 'all or nothing' attitude. If he thought he was going to fail at something, he would avoid it by turning to alcohol rather than facing it head on.

Other characteristics of Type A behaviour include:

- Sense of urgency: Rushing around, feeling that time is against them; always thinking they don't have enough time to spare.
- Impatience/Aggression: Unable to wait in a queue; being rude or aggressive when they perceive others as impeding them in some way. Interrupting others and cutting people off during a discussion.
- Competitive: Constant need to succeed; sense of achievement keeps them going; no room for failure.
- Over-stretched: Taking too much work on at once; always on the go.
- Difficulty switching off: unable to relax; seems full of nervous energy; finds it hard to sleep at night.

Type A behaviour has been linked to physical illnesses such as heart disease, stomach ulcers, and allergies. This sort of personality is especially prevalent in the City which is populated by many perfectionists who mercilessly drive themselves too hard in order to achieve high levels of success. However, if we push ourselves too far, we risk poor mental and physical health.

Tips to overcome Type A behaviour

- What's the rush! Stop dashing around the place and set aside some time to sit down to eat a meal properly. Try and eat away from your desk and leave your Blackberry behind so you aren't tempted to check it every five seconds while you are eating.
- Take a break! Make room in your diary for relaxing activities, like going for a walk or doing relaxation exercises (see Appendices I, II, and III for more ideas!)
- Get a life! Remember: life is not all about work; there has to be some room in there for play too. So take up a hobby that you really enjoy and that will allow you to switch off completely from your working day.
- Try the art of listening! Interrupting others or being rude and aggressive isn't going to win you many friends—at work or at home. Be aware of your own thoughts when others are talking to you and ask yourself if it is really necessary to interrupt them: Is what I have to say important enough to cut them off?
- Face your fears! Type As usually have a major fear of being late. So, in order to overcome this, deliberately turn up a few minutes late for a meeting or hand in work a day past the deadline. Once you realize the world isn't going to come to an end if you're a few minutes late, then you will be able to have a more relaxed attitude towards time.
- Watch your mouth! Be aware of the danger of 'I should' 'I must' or 'I have to'. Replace these thoughts with 'I would like to' or 'I choose to'. Remember: it's not a total crisis if you miss a deadline or fail to get a giant bonus.
- Be sociable! Often perfectionists spend the day glued to their computer screens, afraid to take a break or even visit the bathroom! Make a conscious effort to tear your eyes away from the screen

and go and have a chat to one of your colleagues, about anything other than work! Having a laugh will help you relax and take the pressure off, at least for a few minutes!

- Build relationships! Apart from not interrupting everyone who crosses your path, try and be a bit more appreciative when friends or work colleagues have done something good for you. Type As are often too busy to remember to say 'Thank you' but it is fundamental to acknowledge and praise in order to maintain healthy relationships with others.

- Explore! If you are really having a hard time accessing your 'inner Type A' and making improvements, then think about why you behave the way you do; perhaps it is something to do with the way you were raised. Therapy can help you to understand the reasons for your behaviour and help you to change it accordingly.

The upshot

There is always an underlying reason for unhelpful habits like drinking, drugs, over-eating etc. In many cases, such excessive habits are linked to low self-worth and a lack of confidence. Drinking excessively might be a way to avoid difficult feelings, especially if you are a perfectionist. If we beat ourselves up about our drinking we inevitably lose more confidence, making it harder to deal with what life throws at us, thus a vicious cycle starts to evolve. Once we successfully rebuild our confidence it becomes easier for us to break the cycle, and to beat the habit of dependency once and for all.

CHAPTER FOUR

Hot under the collar

"Speak when you are angry—and you'll make the best speech you'll ever regret."

—Dr. Laurence J Peter

'Oh God, so sorry I'm late. I was stuck behind the slowest driver in the world and he made me late, he was so annoying. The thing is I'm never late; I shouldn't have been. I should have left earlier.'

I looked at this woman called Joanne, who had burst into my office in such a panic and tried to reassure her that it was no problem that she was a few minutes late. To be honest, it had suited me as it had given me a chance to grab a much-needed cup of coffee!

As soon as she calmed down, she rummaged in her bag and whipped out a notebook. With pen poised, eyes fixed on her pad she waited for me to start the session.

'I want to take notes on everything you say,' she told me.

Never before have I seen a patient so proactive and, I must say I was struck by her apparently strong belief that I had all the answers!

Joanne's story

When I asked her why she had come to me, she told me that she had been made redundant from her job as marketing manager for a blue-chip company; that she knew it was because her team had hated her and she wanted to find a way to stop it from ever happening again. Not once, during this whole exchange did she maintain eye contact.

Clearly, she was very upset about being made redundant, as many would be in her position. Some people view redundancy as an opportunity to do other things, especially if the company gives out an excellent redundancy package! However, for the majority of us, being made redundant can understandably affect our self-confidence, self-worth, and self-esteem.

Joanne had taken her redundancy extremely personally. This was the third time in her working life she had been made redundant, so it is not surprising that she felt rejected. She was having a lot of angry outbursts which she felt she couldn't 'control' and she wanted to learn how to stop those angry feelings. She was also having sleepless nights and suffered from very intense pains in her shoulders.

The drill down

Joanne was quite self-aware and told me that she found it difficult to be around other people. In her last job, she had been part of a large team but couldn't bring herself to engage with them in social banter and chit-chat. If people asked about her weekend, or chatted about something on TV or in the papers, she would feel tightness in her chest and pains in her stomach. She only wanted to engage in conversation if it was to do with work.

Outside the loop

Joanne simply didn't trust people. She felt if she revealed anything personal about herself, her work colleagues would use it against her, and try to stop her moving forward in her career.

She wouldn't trust anyone else to do a job properly: never delegated, refused to share work and never, ever, asked for help. There was one situation were Joanne's boss instructed her to delegate parts of a project to one of her team-mates. When the work came back, Joanne was furious that her colleague had not done the work to the same standards as her. She lost her temper in the middle of the office and shouted at her colleague: 'It should have been done this way', 'You don't understand', 'You are totally incompetent'. In one instance, her aggressive behaviour caused a work colleague to cry, but she felt that it was the colleague's fault for being unprofessional.

Following these outbursts of aggressive, verbal behaviour, Joanne would feel very bad and proceed to beat herself up about what had happened, saying to herself: What's wrong with me? I must stop being angry. I hate myself for behaving this way. I can't stop it. However, she couldn't seem to prevent the next explosion from happening.

Because of her strained relationship with her colleagues, she felt that they were conspiring against her and laughing at her behind her back. There was one colleague in particular who she felt was withholding information from her and stealing her clients. All of this meant that she couldn't do her job properly; she felt that her progress and productivity at work was impeded by others which frustrated her intensely. She felt that people didn't understand that she just wanted to be left alone to get on with her job.

The final straw

One day, Joanne was accidentally copied into an email sent by one of her colleagues. The content of it confirmed her worst fears. It described her as a 'nightmare', 'a complete pain to work with' and 'boring'. This absolutely devastated Joanne and led to even more angry outbursts about how unfairly she had been treated. Not long afterwards, Joanne was made redundant. As a result, she felt that her team had conspired together to push her out of her job.

The curse of Type A

Joanne was a perfectionist. Not only did she take notes during our sessions, but asked for homework, twice-weekly meetings and wanted to set a timeframe, detailing exactly how long it would take her to recover. In life, she was very competitive, extremely driven and terrified of failure. She had always felt the need to rush and hurry from one activity and achievement to another and had an overwhelming desire to be successful in all that she did. She found it difficult to relax and constantly felt tense and wound up.

Grassroots

As ever, there was a lot going on in Joanne's personal life. She was married with a three-year-old toddler; the family had just moved house and were in the process of doing it up. A couple of years before, she and her husband had agreed that he would give up his job and stay at home to look after their little girl. They made a deal that he would do the housework, cooking, babysitting etc. while she would be the main breadwinner.

However, the more pressure she felt at work, the angrier she would be when she arrived home. Her husband had put on weight and she felt disgusted by him. She would constantly tell him off for being lazy, criticize him for his weight gain, and demand that he do more exercise. She also felt her husband wasn't doing enough around the house and had failed to deliver on his side of the bargain. As a result, Joanne would spend most of her time either arguing with her husband or re-doing any housework he attempted.

Downsizing

Joanne came from a poor family. Her father spent most of his time working in a neighbouring town and her mother also worked full-time. Her mother was very opinionated and critical of Joanne and would frequently whip her and tell her that she was good for nothing. As a result, Joanne felt she could not do anything right and became very withdrawn. She 'hated' her parents and felt 'misunderstood and rejected' by them.

As a teenager, she immersed herself in academia, an area where she received lots of praise for her efforts. She learned that approval from others seemed to depend on her success and achievements. Furthermore, the more she worked, the less she felt like a failure in her mother's eyes. She realized that she would be able to become independent from her family through study and hard work and, therefore, escape the horrible feelings she felt at home. When she moved into working life, the same rule applied. As long she achieved success in her career, she would be able to feel good about herself and, at the same time, feel that she had escaped the critical comments from her family.

Rising hackles

Anger is one of the first emotions we feel and often the last we learn to manage. It is a natural response designed to protect or defend us from perceived threats to our sense of self-worth. It is often triggered by criticism or a sense of injustice and unfairness; when we feel attacked, put down, rejected, or impeded it would follow that we need to get 'bigger, louder, and stronger' to counteract this experience. Anger is a healthy reaction when expressed productively in a non-aggressive way. It only becomes a problem when it becomes too frequent, too intense, and disrupts our relationships.

Frequent and intense angry outbursts are often a sign of a lack of self-confidence; we may not feel confident to manage the feeling inside us and, therefore, come to rely on anger as an automatic 'coping' mechanism to deal with these uncomfortable feelings. Of course, the more we rely on it, the more we do not give ourselves a unique opportunity to discover that there may be other and more productive ways to cope with these undesirable feelings.

We often think that it is something in our environment that 'makes us angry'; that it's an instantaneous reaction that we can't control. However there are three things that happen when we feel angry:

- The event or incident that we believe influences and acts as a 'trigger' but does not cause our anger.
- An internal dialogue that interprets the event.
- The actual outburst itself, which can lead to physical or aggressive verbal behaviour.

However, there are several ways we can intervene during this process to better manage our anger. Anger management is about gaining insight and a sense of empowerment around this sequence of events.

Chewing nails

When we have angry outbursts, we tend to feel very badly about it afterwards and can become very critical of our behaviour. However, beating ourselves up can affect our self-confidence, which increases the likelihood of more fits of temper. It is a vicious cycle that seems impossible to break.

Joanne was extremely critical of herself and others. Her language was peppered with 'shoulds' and 'musts' and she believed that others caused her anger:

> 'I *must* stop being angry.'
> 'I *should* control myself better.'
> '*If only* people would treat me better.'
> '*If only* mum and dad weren't so difficult.'

All this thinking impacted on her self-confidence. Not only did it enhance her sense of 'failure' but by believing her problem lay outside of her control, it also exacerbated an underlying sense of 'helplessness' in being able to change her experience.

When Joanne was angry she found it very difficult to let grievances go. She would repeat and playback how others mistreated her again and again in her head and envisage scenarios of others mistreating her in a way that might not have even happened. All this mental activity left her feeling even more angry, frustrated, low and helpless.

Anger management

When we feel vulnerable and lack the confidence inside to manage the feeling in relation to our rejection, some part of us, our emotional self, may tend to want to keep the feeling of rejection alive by second-guessing it or repeating it in our mind's eye, so as not to be shocked or 'traumatized' by it unexpectedly in the future.

Angry thoughts are characterized by absolute negative statements often to do with our failings, and the perceived unfairness, injustice and rejection from others. In fact, when we are angry, our language becomes very child-like: 'It's not fair', 'It's all his fault', 'Why is everyone so mean to me?' This sort of language is reflective of child-like feelings of loss or abandonment by not having our basic needs met.

Our thought diaries can, again, come in very handy here. If we can write down and articulate our frustrations, we will be able to stand back from the situation and find new ways of thinking in and around it. We can establish a new perspective and a sense of relief by making a conscious effort to use less absolute and rigid language, for example: the word 'should' could be substituted with 'it would be nice if'.

Similarly, Joanne also realized the benefit of making out a list of advantages and disadvantages of losing her temper as you can see below:

Situation	Advantages of losing temper	Disadvantages of losing temper	Costs of losing temper
Got angry with a work colleague for making a mistake	Feel sense of relief	Still felt tense and wound up afterwards	Full of guilt and feel low about the way I behaved
	Glad I made my point	Felt bad about losing control	Let myself down in front of others.
	Temporary satisfaction when saw colleague upset	After a few minutes felt angry with myself for upsetting her the way I did	Damaged relationship between myself and my colleague

When Joanne made out this list with regards to other situations where she had lost her temper, she realized that getting angry simply wasn't worth the fallout at the other end: the guilt, the self-criticism, and the shame of losing control over her behaviour.

Paradigm shift

We all know that the workplace environment in the City can be highly pressurized and competitive. When we are aggressive, we tend to blame anything, and everyone else for our outbursts rather than accepting responsibility for our own emotional experience and behaviour; it is not others who make us angry but rather ourselves due to the rigid beliefs that we hold and the way we interpret our environment.

In Joanne's case, it was her colleagues that were incompetent, unfriendly and cold. She just wanted to get on with her job! Joanne always thought it was everyone else that had the problem, that nobody understood her. She was completely unaware of how others would perceive her behaviour.

However, the environment itself is not the problem but how we relate to it, make sense of it, and think about it.

Just breathe!

Breathing from the diaphragm is an excellent way to cope with rising anger. When we become angry, we have certain physiological responses from all the adrenalin rushing around our body such as tense shoulders, rigid grinding jaws, and a wrenching feeling in the stomach. Breathing alleviates these physiological effects, and distracts us from our unhelpful thinking, relieves tension, and relaxes us physically and emotionally. (Please refer to Appendices I, II, and III for details of breathing/muscular relaxation exercises.)

First mover advantage

If we express and communicate our anger productively, and in the moment, it can help us in our relationships with others. If we don't express it, we internalize it so it becomes passive for a while. However, our anger stays simmering below the surface until the day comes when we completely explode. A seemingly and usually unchallenging encounter can seem like the 'straw that broke the camel's back!' and others will view our angry behaviour as unwarranted and unjustified, leading to more conflict in the relationship.

The best thing is to address issues as soon as they arise in relationships. If this seems too difficult then we can always readdress the issues at another time; the important thing to remember is that if it is left completely unaddressed, then future issues (that in isolation would not trigger so much anger) will be biased by the emotional memory of the last, and trigger a more intensified outburst.

Usually, when we are angry, as a result of feeling that we have been mistreated, we are actually looking for empathy from others to regain a sense of being understood and validated to counteract that sense of rejection. We can work towards achieving this by using the right language to explain our feelings.

Stay on the level!

It is so important for us to express our anger productively. Joanne constantly chastised her husband for being overweight, lazy, and not doing the housework properly. In turn, he went on a 'passive attack' which led to his inactivity. When she criticized him, he felt that he couldn't do anything right, lost confidence, and simply stopped trying. Conversely, the more inactive her husband became, the more Joanne felt attacked and rejected which, in turn, caused her to be angry and critical.

Every single interaction she had with her husband was a negative one. By expressing our anger and frustrations in a certain way, we can control the situation whilst staying calm.

Joanne came to realise that she also needed to be different in order to create more of the reality that she desired at home with her husband. The problem did not just lay with him alone—they had a shared responsibility to overcome their difficulties. She invited her husband to join us in a couple counselling session to see if they could develop a better way of communicating at home. The following is an example of the helpful communication style that Joanne and her husband developed and practiced together.

They found a way to 'level' with each other, without remaining either aggressive or passive in their communication style. The following statements helped them to air grievances and attend to the emotional experience between them in a more productive manner (please also see Chapter Eight for more communication tips):

The statement's formula that they used is:

I feel 'X', when you do 'Y' as I tend to think 'Z'

Joanne: 'I feel angry when I see you don't wash the floor as I tend to think you don't listen to me or care about keeping the house clean.'

(It is important that Joanne expresses her grievance using the personal word 'I' before explaining how she feels and thinks. If she used the critical word 'you', such as 'you make me angry because you don't care', her husband would feel attacked and would be less inclined to listen to her. Instead, he will simply be thinking of a return attack.)

Joanne's husband can now repeat what she has said back, ensuring that she feels heard.

Husband: 'I heard you say that you feel angry when you see I don't wash the floor, as you think I don't listen to you or care about keeping the house clean. Did I hear you correctly?'

(By repeating the grievance back to Joanne in the same exact words, she can now feel that she is being heard and listened to and has an opportunity to correct him if she still feels unheard. Once she confirms that she has been heard, her husband can validate her experience.)

Husband: 'I understand that you would feel angry when you see I do not wash the floor if you were to think about this as me not listening to you or caring about keeping the house clean.'

(By repeating the grievance once more, Joanne can now feel that she is being understood, validated, and empathized with, but not necessarily agreed with.)

Husband: 'I am sorry that you think and, therefore, feel that way. I didn't realize it bothered you so much. I did not know that you thought of it that way. I will try and be more aware in future.'

By explaining that it is her thoughts and interpretation around her husband's behaviour that have left her feeling angry (rather than her husband himself) he feels less attacked and more inclined to empathize with her. It also gives him an opportunity to learn how to influence her anger and help their relationship in the future.

Once both parties are happy with the outcome of the discussion, they can switch places. Thus, Joanne's husband was then able to have a chance to air his particular grievance.

This style of communication allows for difference in opinion and perspective on the same issue. Her husband can also express his grievance in a non-attacking manner. The objective of this communication style is not to prove your partner wrong or try to change their point of view in line with yours, but to validate each other's experiences around the same situation, accepting, yet not necessarily agreeing, with each other's different point of view.

It is also important to follow up each grievance with a positive statement, for example:

'I felt fantastic the other day when I saw you got up early to put out the bins as I really thought that you cared about keeping the house tidy.'

Remember, it's always the little things that can lead to angry outbursts. We feel that if someone doesn't pull their weight around the house that they don't care or respect our feelings. Our partners, work colleagues etc. cannot read our minds. If there is something they do that makes us feel annoyed or even happy, it is important for us to communicate this to them; if we don't or if we assume that they should know how their behaviour influences our experience then we our doing ourselves no favours at all! It is our responsibility to create more of the reality that we desire, not to wait for, or to expect others to do that for us!

Dividing the spoils: Delegation

One of Joanne's major problems at work was her inability to delegate. She simply didn't trust her team enough to get the job done well and feared it would reflect badly on her when they made mistakes. However, because she insisted on doing everything herself, she ended up overworked, frustrated, tired, and angry.

Delegation is not about offloading the uninteresting work to someone else, but to give others the opportunity to do work that will develop their skills and help them grow in confidence. For a team to function to its optimal level, each member must have as many skills as possible in order for the work to get done efficiently and to the highest standard. It is poor team management to be as proprietary about work as Joanne and her approach led to her colleagues resenting her for it.

Benefits of delegation

Effective delegation can have the following advantages:

- Frees up more time to focus on more important tasks
- Encourages interaction with team
- Helps others learn and develop new skills
- Gets the group working as a team

Coveting the work

There are many reasons why people are reluctant to delegate. In Joanne's case, she was afraid of letting go and losing control; she ultimately feared failure and rejection. She also took some satisfaction in being a 'martyr', feeling very 'good' about herself that she didn't need anyone's help, and that nobody but her could do the work well. She also took pride in the fact that she never delegated. Of course, Joanne was a perfectionist and didn't trust anyone else to do the work. She saw delegation as a sign of weakness—an admission that she wasn't coping.

However, there are other reasons why we don't delegate. We might feel bad about asking our team members to take on work, especially if they appear really busy. Or maybe there is that fear that if we delegate work, then that person might mess it up, which will reflect badly on us. Conversely, we might also be secretly scared that the other person will do a better job than ourselves and pass us out on the career ladder.

Have a look at the following statements and see if any of them seem familiar:

- I'd be better off doing it myself
- They won't do it as well as I will
- I will look weak and lazy if I delegate
- Everyone else has too much on; they don't need more work
- They might do a better job than myself
- I won't have control over the task if I delegate

In such a competitive environment, it is understandable that most of us will have experienced at least one or two of these thoughts at one point or another. However, learning how to delegate effectively will help to minimize those fears and give you the confidence to manage your workload in a way that best suits your needs.

How to delegate

Set the task

This does not mean spelling out every single part of the task, but setting the objective: why the job needs to get done; what the end goal should be; and how much time they have to complete the job.

Choose your audience

Consider who is right for the type of work you are allocating. Just because Jim did a great job last time doesn't mean that you need to give him all the jobs in the future. Similarly, if Kate messed up on a previous task, then that's no reason to avoid her either. Play to the individual's skills and really think about who is suitable for the task at hand.

Give it up

Make sure you give the entire project to the other person and allow them to be fully responsible for the job. Only allocating part of a task implies that you don't entirely trust the person (which you may not) but will bring about its own problems.

Share the wealth

Make sure that you give the team equal opportunities to do the work by spreading it around. This will help them to develop their skills and give them new experiences.

Monitor progress

This does not mean looking over their shoulder every five minutes. Instead, set interim deadlines and arrange regular updates, so you can both have a chat about how things are progressing. It also helps to ensure that the team member still has a clear idea of their objectives.

Give feedback

When the task is finished, sit down, and go through it with the team member. Make sure you praise the parts that were successfully completed. If there were areas that you felt could have been done better, then make your comments clear and constructive, so they will be able to learn from them.

Relationships at home

Joanne made an effort to spend more time with her husband and child. Rather than focusing on cleaning the whole house from top to bottom every night, she decided to only do a little bit at a time. This made her feel more relaxed and left her more free to enjoy spending time with her loved ones.

If she feels annoyed by something she will catch herself and voice her experience assertively rather than remaining passive or becoming aggressive. She has made an effort to be kinder and more appreciative of her husband's efforts and to spend quality time with him. They have also fixed a certain time every week to air their respective grievances through the use of levelling statements.

Relationships at work

Joanne learned that her cold, distant, and aggressive behaviour was not a healthy way to form relationships. Being so abrupt with her colleagues made them feel vulnerable and defensive and so they went on the attack. She became aware that people wouldn't do what she wanted when she was aggressive.

Usually, if we think someone doesn't like us, it can make us feel rejected and bad about ourselves. Thus, we tend to seek comfort and validation from others. Once we get a few like-minded people on board, we can end up ganging up on a particular individual. This is what happened in Joanne's team. She was aggressive with others and they went on the attack.

Getting on with people is fundamental to a healthy working environment. Sometimes it is even more important to fit into the team than doing the job.

Anger management tips

- If you start feeling angry about something, and you feel too incensed to react calmly, then simply get up and walk away from the situation. Find a safe spot and punch a pillow or head down to the basement and scream out your frustration! This will help you to vent your anger and put you in a better mood to deal with the problem in a calm and rational manner.
- Breathing deeply and doing relaxation and meditation exercises are great ways to help you feel calm and in control. (Please refer to Appendices I, II, and III for examples of breathing, meditation, and relaxation exercises.)
- Counting to ten does sound like a bit of a cliché but it does work! The next time you feel like you are going to lose your temper, then start counting. If that doesn't work, then keep on counting and breathing until you feel in a better state to deal with the situation.
- Taking a break or going for a walk is also a good way to distract yourself from your anger. Getting some physical distance from the problem will allow you to think about it in a calmer and more rational way. Then when you return, you will more likely be in a better position to find a resolution.
- Challenging your thoughts is also a great way to prevent you from making a mountain out of a molehill. Joanne came to realize that: 'It's not the end of the world that I was made redundant. If my anger was a factor then I will take steps to address it, then I will do my best to find another job.'
- Being aware how the language you use is fundamental when challenging your core beliefs. For example, we often believe that others 'make' us angry, or they 'should' behave in a certain way. It is important that we know that nobody can 'make' us feel anything. Anger is about the way we interpret a situation and react to it. Similarly, replacing the 'shoulds' with 'it would be better if' or 'I would prefer it if' is a good way of challenging the rigidity of our beliefs, and relieving the rising tension.
- Thinking alternative and less rigid thoughts is key for overcoming those feelings of anger. Outbursts of anger often result when we take things personally. For example, when Joanne would see

the team chatting together in another room, she would think they were conspiring against her. However, she began to see the merit in making alternative self-statements such as: 'They are working on a deadline and most probably talking about work; the chances are this has nothing to do with me'; or 'Maybe they are talking about me, but I will treat this as a challenge and remain calm when I address them about how I am feeling.' This positive self-talk is really a preventative measure that allows us to stay in control.

- Avoiding the problem will not make it go away. If we let problems build up, then it is more likely that we will end up losing our temper. Try and address the situation head on; the sooner it is resolved, the better you will feel.
- Communicating in a non-attacking way is fundamental towards expressing our anger in a healthy manner. Using assertive statements such as 'I feel angry because ...' is far more effective than using 'blame statements' against someone else for the way we feel.
- Losing our temper can be a culmination of different types of stressors in our lives. Poor diet and a '24/7' work ethic can affect the way we behave and leave us feeling wound up. Leading a healthy lifestyle and achieving a work/life balance will have more positive affects on our mood and state of mind.

The upshot

Joanne was able to manage her anger and relationships in order to create more of the reality that she wanted: more understanding and empathy, and less 'rejection'. As a result she felt more confident and behaved more assertively; she began to trust in others and relationships more. Her new and improved levels of confidence led her to feel more relaxed and less fearful of failure and rejection.

Anger is not a bad thing; it is a normal, human reaction. It would be unrealistic to think that we should never be angry; holding this belief will only lead to a sense of failure. There are several ways to manage our anger and use it more productively.

The competitive and critical nature of the City's working environments, understandably, leads to vulnerabilities around our self-worth; it would follow that we may take a defensive angry position to protect ourselves. However, we can get into a vicious cycle of anger due to low self-confidence and sensitivity around unresolved and intense emotions. Once we are able to channel these intense emotions in different ways then we can learn to be more assertive in our communication whilst also empathizing with the experience of others. By managing our anger productively, we will find that we are getting what we want from others, and enjoying our working relationships once again.

CHAPTER FIVE

Uncomfortably numb

"There are some people who live in a dream world, and there are some who face reality, and then there are those who turn one into the other."

—Douglas H Everett

Consider what you would think if a friend or family member described the following to you:

'I feel a bit weird: separate from the world like I am living in a dream or I am an actor watching my life play out on stage; sort of robot-like and my head feels like it is full of cotton-wool.'

Be honest: you would think they were nuts, right? To be fair, you would be forgiven for edging away nervously, and making a run for the nearest exit.

Now, have a look at the next scenario:

You are driving along a country road in your fancy Porsche going a zillion miles per hour and loving it. Suddenly, an unexpected tight corner appears; you slam on the brakes and the

79

car does a violent skid, spinning you around and then upside
down. You find yourself upturned, in a ditch.

During the skid, you might have felt that everything was going
around in slow motion, or felt a bit unreal or numb. When you got
out of the car, you may feel a bit detached from everything or that
your voice is coming from very far away. It is only later when you
come back 'to reality' that you might notice that you're bleeding or
that your hands are shaking.

Perhaps you would agree that these sensations of feeling a bit 'out of it' aren't a million miles away from what your
friend described to you. However, prolonged or more intense
feelings of detachment are symptomatic of a condition called
depersonalization.

Depersonalization is not nuts!

I wanted to highlight depersonalization as I'm seeing more and
more cases of it; especially amongst those who are under a lot of
pressure in the City workplace. Depersonalization is usually linked
to anxiety and worry (please see Chapter Two for more on anxiety
and worry) and is far more common than we think. The problem is
that it is still a widely unknown disorder which means that people
tend to hide it away and keep it secret for fear of others thinking
they are insane.

As in the example of the car skidding, it may come as a surprise
that all of us experience sensations associated with depersonalization at one time or another; not only in traumatic situations, but
also when we are tired, hung-over, or feeling pressured by work
demands. Most of us will get spots in front of our eyes, feel a bit 'out
of it', or that our head is full of straw .... These are familiar feelings
for all of us, but it doesn't mean we are crazy! People with depersonalization simply experience these sensations more intensely and, in
some cases, for longer periods of time.

It is an incredibly scary and debilitating experience and if left
undiagnosed and untreated sufferers can live in a constant state of
fear and discomfort. Understandably, many sufferers do seek help,
believing that they may have a brain abnormality or some other
severe and chronic physical disorder.

Jim's story

Jim is a 24-year-old assistant trader. He has only been in his job a few months and knows he has to prove himself. In fact, his situation is even more stressful as it is the height of the credit crunch and he knows jobs like his are few and far between. In his short time, Jim has watched colleagues on the trading desk being marched out of the building. Due to the unspoken 'last-in-first-out' company policy, Jim knows there is a good chance his head will be on the chopping block if it comes to cutting employees. He is terrified of being made redundant and starts to work longer and longer hours to prove that he is an asset to the company.

It is a busy job, and being 'on the ball' is paramount. The busier he gets the more overwhelmed he becomes and starts to feel a sense of disengagement from others at work. During conversations with his colleagues, he doesn't feel present; like he is outside himself—and completely numb. When he feels like this, he worries that others will pick up on it and think him stupid and incompetent. His sense of anxiety around work increases and he is very concerned about his ability to function at work. His concentration is poor and he is unable to remember things.

A few weeks into his job, one of his desk-mates asks him to go for a drink. Jim reluctantly agrees. While he is in the bar with his friend, Jim begins to check how he is feeling inside; he finds that he is not enjoying himself as much as he 'should' be and begins to get that numb, 'out of body' sensation: that the world looks two-dimensional, flat, painted, made of paper—and that he is on auto-pilot.

Terrified his friend will notice he has 'zoned-out' of the conversation, he makes his excuses and leaves. Jim turns down all social invitations after that.

Over a period of time, Jim begins to experience these unpleasant sensations more and more often. He starts questioning his life and becomes very philosophical about his place in the world; why he is here and if he even exists at all. He repeatedly checks his reflection in mirrors to see if he is still there—and his work colleagues tease him about being vain.

The more anxious he becomes the less he sleeps and despite staying late to check, and double check, his work over and over again, he still makes mistakes.

When his colleagues gently point out a couple of minor mistakes in his work, Jim goes to pieces and has a violent panic attack. This prompts him to seek help.

Hannah's story

When Hannah came to me, she told me that everything in the world seemed distorted and changed shape. She even told me that my head appeared to be stretched, like a cartoon character. Hannah also had a problem feeling physical sensations. When she banged her head, she felt nothing. Similarly, when she made love with her partner, she would feel numb, as if she was floating outside herself. She explained that she had a pervading sense of numbness, of not feeling grounded, as if her whole life was just an act.

It turned out that Hannah had a, seemingly, impeccable track history. She came from a very privileged background, excelled in school, and graduated from a top university. As extremely success-ful actors, her parents were big characters and seldom out of the public eye. As an only child, they were overprotective and very involved in her life from as early as she could remember. At the age of five, she began her acting career; starring in ads and playing small parts in her parents' films. Growing up, she was always with them, and accompanied them to movie premieres and celebrity events. She regarded her parents as her best friends and even hung out with their pals, rather than mixing with friends of her own age.

As she grew older, Hannah began to enjoy school far more than acting. She told her parents she wanted to become a lawyer. Her par-ents dismissed this idea and pushed her further into acting. Hannah was always a 'good child' and felt unable to challenge her parents' life-plan for her.

When Hannah was sixteen, she, unknowingly, accepted a hash brownie from one of her father's famous friends while she was at a club. She tripped out, collapsed, and had to be carried home. As she was being put to bed, she was horrified to see that her father's face was blurred and misshapen. Terrified by her experience, she vowed never to touch drugs again. Although the incident wasn't her fault, she felt that her parents blamed her for being naïve and stupid. However, she felt the 'trip' she had experienced was a one-off, and she put it down to the drugs she had taken.

A few days later, Hannah was on the set of her latest film when she began to experience the same unreal feelings. Mortified, she burst out crying in front of the whole crew and was sent home. When she tried to talk to her parents about the episodes and how she was feeling, they dismissed her, telling her not to be so stupid; she was just 'imagining things' and she sounded like a 'crazy person'. Her father told her he had 'no time' for people who claimed they had mental problems. When she appealed to her mother, she was simply told not to 'upset' her father by saying such strange things. However, they reluctantly agreed to allow her to take a break from acting, and she returned to school.

Hannah studied hard and made it into a prestigious university where she studied law. Disappointed that she was not following in their footsteps, her parents gradually withdrew from her and communication became stilted and uncomfortable.

When she graduated, Hannah moved to the City and after a few years of intensive work, managed to become partner in a law firm. She married a fellow lawyer, had two children and, from the outside, looked like she led a charmed life. However, since her first hallucinations at the age of sixteen, Hannah still had constant feelings of distorted reality and numbness and was finding it more and more difficult to cope with them. She was overwhelmed with guilt as she did not feel anything for her husband or her children. She felt her whole life was about going through the motions, acting like she felt affection for them when all she felt was numbness. Her symptoms had a massive effect on her work and her home life and she was terrified she would be 'found out' and that others would notice her inattentiveness and how detached she was from her environment.

For twenty years, she hid her symptoms, terrified that her friends and work colleagues would think she was crazy, just as her parents believed.

The low down

There is no known reason for depersonalization—why some people get it and others don't. It has been linked to anxiety and those that experience panic attacks also appear to be susceptible. In the past, it was especially prevalent among concentration camp victims. However, there is no evidence to suggest it is hereditary.

Depersonalization is more common in younger people (early teens to mid-twenties) but it can also be experienced at any age.

Back in the day, depersonalization used to be confused with schizophrenia. Even now, misdiagnoses still occur. Although depersonalization is becoming more common, there is not a lot of knowledge out there, even in the medical field. I have personally seen depersonalization misdiagnosed as depression, schizophrenia, and other psychotic disorders. The main distinction between depersonalization and schizophrenia is the use of the phrase: 'It's as if'. Patients with depersonalization feel 'as if' the world is unreal, flat; whilst schizophrenics feel that everything *is* artificial. Or 'It's as if this voice isn't mine', as opposed to 'it *is* that this voice isn't mine'.

So, although we don't really know the cause of depersonalization, we do know that there are certain factors that may trigger its onset or recurrent episodes:

• Artificial light
• Crowds
• Drugs (such as cannabis, LSD, ecstasy)
• Alcohol
• Over-exercising
• Tiredness, lack of sleep or insomnia
• Severe emotional problems
• Heightened episodes of anxiety and panic
• Stressful and demanding situations at work
• Traumatic life events (such as death, relationship break-ups, redundancy)

There is also no firm pattern to depersonalization. Some people will experience short episodes lasting hours or a couple of days, whilst others might have a constant sense of strange sensations that grow worse when dealing with stressful situations.

Freeze, flight or fight

In times of anxiety, our bodies are designed to exert a fight or flight response to help us cope with stressful situations (please see Chapter One for more information on flight and flight responses). But we could say that depersonalization provokes a freeze-like response: mentally rolling up into a ball to avoid getting hurt. Usually, when we are confronted with emotional trauma, our bodies produce a huge amount of adrenalin which enables us to either flee the scene or stand our ground. In the case of depersonalization, it may be more about floating above the situation. It is as if our subconscious-self may be trying to separate ourselves from the potential reoccurrence of emotional trauma in stressful situations. However, in the long term this is pretty unproductive for our conscious experience.

The world is flat

There are many aspects to depersonalization and symptoms can overlap in many cases. Both Jim and Hannah experienced strong feelings of derealisation—feeling that the world is artificial and unreal—and deaffectualization—a sense that you are unable to feel things emotionally.

Deaffectualization is characterized and often maintained by constant self-scrutinization. In Jim's case, he would constantly check in with himself to examine his own level of enjoyment and constantly ask himself questions like: 'Am I happy?' 'Am I enjoying myself?' 'Am I having as good an experience as I did last time?'

Of course, when Jim checks to see how happy he is, he is less grounded and more distracted from the moment. Constant checking increases the likelihood of Jim not getting any enjoyment from the event he is supposed to be engaging in. A vicious cycle starts to emerge and evolve—the more he worries about how he is not enjoying himself, the more he will feel detached from any potential enjoyment of the moment and then the more anxious he will become. When Jim finds himself less happy than he 'should' be, he feels like a failure, and his anxiety increases further as a result.

Like Jim, Hannah also experienced moments of derealisation along with her feelings of depersonalization and desomatization (unable to physically feel anything). The distorted reality she experienced (faces stretching etc.), was a result of the rush of adrenalin in her body which blurred her vision and caused disturbing hallucinations. (Please refer to Chapter Two for a diagram on the physical effects of anxiety.)

Get grounded!

Grounding techniques can be extremely useful in tethering you to the moment:

The world around you

Consciously taking in your surroundings in great detail is a way of engaging with your external environment. Note down what you can see, hear, feel, smell and touch. By constantly asking yourself questions about what's around you, you will feel more grounded in the present, and more in the moment.

Grounding language

The language we use is extremely important when we are trying to overcome a particular problem. Positive statements can really make a difference when we are trying to quell those feelings of anxiety. Repeating the following statements will really help to calm those feelings of depersonalization:

- I will get better if I keep trying
- I am strong and I can cope with this
- These uncomfortable feelings will soon go away
- I have the support that will help me through this

It is helpful to write down these statements. Hannah used to note down her own personal desires on post-it notes and paste them all over her house! Whatever method you choose, ensure that you have access to these statements, whether you memorize them or have them written down.

Distracting yourself

Shifting your focus is invaluable when tackling feelings of depersonalization. Write down some of your favourite hobbies and things to do and refer back to the list when you start experiencing unsettling feelings. For example, Hannah loved gossiping on the phone, listening to music, and painting. When she explored these activities, she was able to distract herself from her feelings of depersonalization. (Please refer to Chapter Two for more information and tips about distraction).

The man in the mirror

Obsessively looking in the mirror is another aspect of self-scrutinization. Jim would constantly check that he was there but the more he stares the more out of it he feels; that it's not him in the reflection, and that he is watching from outside himself, and this causes him a great deal of anxiety. However, not everyone with depersonalization looks repeatedly in the mirror: for example, Hannah was too scared to look in the mirror for fear of not seeing her own reflection.

The thing is: even if we all stared into the mirror for a good length of time, most of us would feel that weird out of body sensation. However, people with depersonalization tend to attribute symptoms which they would usually think were normal, to their illness. For example, if we wake up in the morning, most of us will get that 'not quite there' feeling. If those with depersonalization feel that way, they think they are having another episode. (Please see Chapter One for more on selective bias in our thinking.)

By checking in to see how 'depersonalized' we are, we more often than not, conclude the worst by misinterpreting understandable bodily sensations in catastrophic terms. This can exacerbate our anxiety and increase the likelihood of having another episode of depersonalization.

By applying the grounding methods described above we can combat these unpleasant feelings of depersonalization, and avoid mentally checking in. For example:

- Use positive cognitive coping statements: 'It is undesirable to feel this way but I can cope. If I worry less about it, it will pass sooner.' And 'I may not feel 100% right now but that is ok, I can still get some enjoyment from spending time with my friends'.
- Try and avoid staring in the mirror.
- Distract yourself by focusing on other more pleasurable pursuits (calling a friend, listening to music etc.)
- Think, plan, but don't worry about the day ahead ...
- Breathe! (Please see Appendix I for more on breathing exercises)

These exercises will help you to feel in the moment and will prevent you from feeling as if you are 'floating away' from reality.

Circling back

Depersonalization is often found in those with a history of feeling anxious, and have a tendency to worry and/or be rather philosophical about 'why we are here' or have anxiety about the world ending. It is also often found in those who have experienced emotional childhood trauma. Childhood abuse often triggers the symptoms but also parental over-protectiveness or neglect can play a part. In Hannah's case, her parents were too involved in her life. They were big characters who constantly stole the limelight and, thus, Hannah was never allowed the freedom to develop her own personality, sense of autonomy and self-confidence. Whenever Hannah tried to assert her individuality, she was shouted down and 'set on the right path'.

Depersonalization can affect those who are starved of the right sort of attention. When they are not allowed to express themselves, they tend to feel under pressure to be something they're not. For Hannah, depersonalization may be the manifestation of a subconscious need to separate herself and show that she is an individual. She felt misunderstood and that her condition wasn't real. In some respects, for her, depersonalization may be a way of dealing with some unresolved feelings around a past sense of rejection. We may be looking for attention or want to be recognized as an individual. With depersonalization, those around us are forced to stop and listen, and understand that our feelings are real and what we are suffering from is a very real condition.

Addressing those statements

'I'd rather have a broken leg'

Depersonalization is a very intangible condition and difficult for others to understand. Everyone has heard of depression but there isn't a lot out there about depersonalization. Contrary to what many sufferers believe, depersonalization largely goes unnoticed by others. They cannot tell whether you are feeling depersonalized. They may notice that you are a little distracted but that's generally the extent of it.

Because sufferers look fine and appear to be functioning and acting normally, it is understandable that friends, family, and work colleagues do not suspect that something is wrong.

This is frustrating for sufferers of depersonalization and they can become depressed as a result. Therefore, sufferers tend to keep their condition hidden, hoping it will go away.

However, the very act of discussing depersonalization can have a positive therapeutic effect on the sufferer. Many of those with depersonalization don't think the condition is real, but knowing that others experience it, and also understanding the reasons behind it brings about a tremendous sense of relief. For example, Hannah was so frustrated with her parents' attitude that she persuaded her father to come to one of our sessions. With a little guidance from me (using the levelling statement formula from Chapter Three) the dialogue went something like this:

Hannah: 'I feel anxious when I hear you tell me that I am imagining things and I should get over it. I think that you don't understand me or appreciate what is important to me.'

Father: 'I heard you say that you feel anxious when you hear me tell you that you are imagining things and to get over it as you think I don't understand or appreciate what is important to you.'

Father: 'I understand how you would feel anxious if you hear me tell you that you are imagining things and to get over it, if you think I am not appreciating what is important to you—that makes sense to me.'

As we have seen in Chapter Three, the dialogue continues until both parties feel empathized with, and understand each other, and the emotional consequences of their thoughts about each other's behaviours.

By deliberately choosing to use expressions such as 'I hear' and 'I understand', indicates that you are willing to listen to the other person and that you are trying to understand what they are going through.

Despite being a chronic sceptic about mental illness, Hannah's father began to understand that his daughter had a very real condition and that she wasn't just 'making it up' or being 'dramatic'.

With the help of her family and friends, Hannah began to feel better and her feelings of depersonalization gradually abated.

Expressing how you feel to your friends or family is difficult, but if both parties learn to phrase it in the right way, it can really help to improve communication.

Tips for friends and family

It takes a lot of courage to admit feelings of 'going insane' to friends and family. A lack of understanding from loved ones can make the sufferer feel hopeless and alone. So here are some tips on how to handle friends or family that are experiencing symptoms of depersonalization:

Do's and Don'ts for Friends and Family:

- Do take the person's concerns seriously.
- Don't ignore them; lend an empathic ear and listen to what they are saying.
- Do show you are listening and understanding them by repeating back what they are saying in their own words.
- Don't offer solutions, unhelpful reassurance or assume you understand by using phrases like: 'It's all in your head' 'You're just a bit stressed' and 'Pull yourself together'.
- Do help them to seek treatment, preferably with a professional who knows about depersonalization.
  Don't dismiss and ignore them and hope the problem will go away.

'I hate going to social gatherings'

Both Hannah and Jim went out of their way to avoid difficult situations. They turned down social invitations and hid themselves away for fear of being 'found out'. Hannah, in particular, found that alcohol made her feel worse and tended to 'trigger' an episode, so that gave her another excuse to avoid social gatherings. However, avoidance simply worsens the condition (please see Chapter One and Chapter Two for more on 'avoidant' behaviours); for example, both Jim and Hannah admitted that they felt lonely which led to feelings of sadness and depression which only served to heighten their sensations of depersonalization.

However, gradual exposure helps reduce the anxiety you associate with these situations. It is important that you set achievable goals. Setting goals that are too demanding may lead to a sense of failure, especially if you are the type of person who tends to beat themselves up when they don't meet their targets. Of course, you will feel anxious at the beginning but you will gradually build enough confidence to confront your fears and you will notice your symptoms lessen as time goes by.

Jim found it helpful to list the social situations he feared and had been avoiding. He rated them on a scale of 1 to 10 (1 = mild depersonalization, 10 = extreme depersonalization)

This is a snapshot of Jim's list of uncomfortable situations:

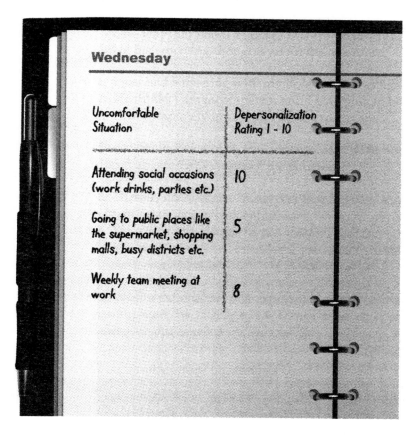

Wednesday	
Uncomfortable Situation	Depersonalization Rating 1 - 10
Attending social occasions (work drinks, parties etc.)	10
Going to public places like the supermarket, shopping malls, busy districts etc.	5
Weekly team meeting at work	8

It is important to choose a situation that has a rating of no more than 4 or 5 from this list. Any situation with a higher rating may seem too difficult to manage at first and lower ratings may not be challenging enough to tackle.

Jim first chose 'going to public places'. As a first step on the road to gradually introducing himself to an uncomfortable situation, he sat quietly and imagined himself in the supermarket, using all his senses to imagine the crowds and capture all the other sights and smells around him. He was aware of his anxiety and depersonalization rising but he refused to give into his panicky feelings. Instead, he used helpful coping mechanisms to reduce his feelings of depersonalization such as breathing, grounding, and helpful self-talk (i.e., my anxiety and depersonalization will pass; this is unpleasant but I can cope).

Once Jim noticed how his anxiety and feelings of depersonalization decreased, he started to feel more mentally prepared to tackle this situation in real life. When he did so, he was able to rely on the tried and tested coping techniques he had used to manage his depersonalization when visualising the scenario.

Obviously, for Jim, a mark of 10 indicates extreme anxiety around mixing with others in social situations. However, it helps to break down the situation by setting realistic goals and tackling manageable small steps. Taking on the entirety of the feared situation will only seem overwhelming and exacerbate a sense of 'failure'. For example: Jim could set a goal to go along to a social gathering such as a 'work drinks' and stay for half an hour. Then the following week, he could stay a little bit longer etc., The more he practices mixing with others, the more confident and less anxious he will feel.

It is important, however, that when Jim does mix with others he tries to distract himself from worrying about his depersonalization and avoids checking in with how he is feeling. (Please refer to the distraction techniques outlined in Chapter Two.) Furthermore, he could also start to collate evidence to prove that others did not notice his depersonalization, and how they seemed interested in what he was saying to them.

If Jim goes along to these events without being mindful of his thoughts, and without his 'tool bag' of helpful coping techniques, they will only exacerbate his problem. Worrying and self-scrutinising at social gatherings will simply be doing more of the same to intensify his problem—remember it's not what we do but *how* we do it that is important.

As Jim practised gradually exposing himself to situations he feared, he found his anxiety and related depersonalization lessening. Over time, he began to feel more comfortable and confident.

Each time Jim confronted his fears he went back to his diary and re-rated his experience. He soon noticed that over a period of time, his ratings reduced and he felt less anxious about confronting certain situations.

'I feel like I'm back to square one'

Like many mental health conditions, depersonalization is complicated by rather high self-expectations particularly around recovery times and coping with the condition. Thus, there is a lot of self-criticism and a preoccupation with how sufferers feel they 'should' be. They focus on what they are not rather than what they are. They can become frustrated, low, and anxious about the seemingly slow progress they may be making which will only exacerbate their depersonalization.

When the problem is revealed, there is an expectation of instant recovery. When this doesn't happen, the sufferer mentally beats himself up for not being able to cope and feels that they are 'back to square one' again. (Please see Chapter One for more information about developing self-acceptance around recovery.)

Many sufferers find it difficult to recover from their experience with depersonalization. They feel they can't move forward because of the memories associated with their condition. This means that when they become anxious during 'normal' events such as giving a presentation to senior management or getting a shock when a car hoots its horn as they cross the road, they attribute these anxious feelings with depersonalization. In many cases, they become obsessed with how they are feeling, focusing on what's going on inside them rather than what's happening outside. This further reinforces the feelings of being detached or cut off from reality.

Consider this internal monologue that Jim describes when he is in a meeting with his boss:

> *I'm getting that weird feeling again. Oh God, now it's getting worse. Everything is unreal, distorted. I'm not here. It's like I'm behind a pane of glass. My boss is talking to me but I'm not listening. I can hear myself answer him back but I have no idea what I am saying or even if it is me saying it. My voice feels very far away.*
>
> *Now he's going to know I'm not paying attention and he's going to think I am stupid. What's happening to me? Am I going mad? Is there something wrong with my brain? Am I schizophrenic?*

Of course, Jim emerges from the meeting shaken and panicky. He hasn't absorbed any of the information from the meeting which further intensifies his anxiety. As a result, he feels he can't manage his feelings and the episode is prolonged.

One way Jim could manage this traumatic situation is to write down his worrying thoughts about the situation:

1. I just had a meeting with my boss and it was terrible.
2. He thinks I am incompetent and I am going to be fired.
3. I am completely insane and no use to anyone.

The above is the worst-case scenario. But what about if Jim introduced an alternative view of the situation?

1. There is no evidence to suggest that my boss suspected my inattention or lack of concentration.
2. Even if he did, maybe he just thinks I am having a bad day.
3. Maybe it's ok to feel this way in times of anxiety. It doesn't make me a crazy person.

When Jim rationalizes his experience and challenges his negative assumptions, he is able to see things more clearly and, over time, learns to cope better with his anxiety.

'I constantly check my feelings'

Depersonalization sufferers are prone to constant self-monitoring which means they become more introverted and less engaged with the world. Diary keeping is a great way of externalising those internal feelings. By monitoring the triggers and associated strength of the symptoms you can measure the effect and the impact they have on your daily life. For example: if you find yourself anxious wedged in amongst the crowds on the Tube then record it. Write down your thoughts and behaviours and associated feelings and symptoms at the time. This will help you to notice how certain thoughts and behaviours lead to feelings of anxiety and symptoms of depersonalization. You can start to monitor your thoughts, behaviours and associated feelings and notice how they affect your symptoms. Once a pattern has been established, you can begin to address your feelings of depersonalization.

You can record and monitor the pattern of thoughts and behaviours that increase feelings of anxiety and symptoms of depersonalization like Jim has done below:

Situation	Symptoms of Depersonalization/ Intensity of symptom (1-10)	Anxiety Level (1 -10)	Thoughts Affecting Anxiety and Depersonalization	Behaviours Affecting Anxiety and Depersonalization
On the crowded Tube	Feeling like I'm outside of my body (9)	(8)	"I feel like this is not my body" "Am I really here?" "I feel like I am floating above myself" "Other people think I'm weird" "I can't stop this feeling" "I'm going insane" "I can't feel the handle in my hand" "I can't feel my eyebrows moving"	Squeezing on tighter to the handle. Moving my eyebrows up and down

Once you have identified thoughts and behaviours that seem to go towards increasing you anxiety and depersonalization you can try and do less of them next time you are in the same situation.

Again, in the same way as Jim has done below, record your diary entry like this:

Situation	Symptoms of Depersonalization/ Intensity of symptom (1-10)	Anxiety Level (1 -10)	Thoughts Affecting Anxiety and Depersonalization	Behaviours Affecting Anxiety and Depersonalization
On the crowded Tube	Feeling like I'm outside of my body (4)	(5)	"This is my body and I am definitely here on the tube". "I am not going insane, I am feeling anxious and these feelings will pass if I worry and check myself less". "Nobody has noticed me, they are all busy reading newspapers".	Holding the handle less tightly. Not moving my eyebrows up and down. Distracting my worry by reading the adverts on the tube. Distracting my worry by listening to music on my ipod

The self-scrutinising aspect of depersonalization can be debilitating in itself. Therefore, it is good to write down some ways you can distract yourself from this obsessive behaviour. For example: commit to going for a walk every day, and notice all the sights and sounds around you, or call up a friend for a chat. Anything that shifts the mental focus from your own self-monitoring will help you to reintegrate with the world around you.

Other treatment

Medication

Some medication such as anti-depressants may exacerbate the condition. Side-effects associated with anti-depressants include: nausea, dizziness, headaches, shaking etc., and can often be misinterpreted as depersonalization which can make the sufferer feel even more anxious. However, if side-effects can be tolerated and not misinterpreted in catastrophic terms, some medications have proven successful in the treatment of depersonalization.

Diet

As with all anxiety-related disorders, depersonalization can bring about a surge of adrenalin in our systems. Adrenalin-enhancing elements include: drugs, caffeine and alcohol. Thus, it is best if you remove these from your diet. Apart from being bad for you, they can also affect your sleep and make the sufferer think they are having another episode.

Exercise

Similarly, too much exercise can worsen the condition because of the amount of adrenalin produced. Any of us might feel breathless, floaty or light-headed after vigorous exercise. However, depersonalization sufferers may attribute these feelings to their condition and worry about them, which can aggravate the problem. Keeping active is important but it is best to avoid running too many marathons especially at the beginning of treatment.

The upshot

Both Hannah and Jim managed to cope with their feelings of depersonalization and gradually began to feel more real and engaged with the world. Both agreed that telling others about how they were feeling was the first step to recovery. After a short period of absence, they returned to work, and by following the exercises described above, found ways to control their anxiety.

Depersonalization is still a bit of an anomaly, but thanks to the internet and greater awareness amongst the medical community, more and more sufferers are coming forward to seek help.

The City work environment is demanding, competitive, and critical. It can seem unforgiving and does not allow for any weaknesses. Many City workers may tend to look in on themselves and self-scrutinize in the hope of bettering themselves to ensure success and survival. Remember: too much of anything, particularly a harsh and critical self-monitoring thinking style may, at times, lead to feelings of anxiety and heightened psychological distress.

CHAPTER SIX

Force of habit

"When eating an elephant take one bite at a time"
—Creighton Abrams

R ecently, a very pale, dangerously thin, girl called Lucy walked meekly into my office. She sat down, fiddled with the end of her coat and told me through a wave of long hair that she was having problems with time management (Please see Chapter Nine for more information on Time Management). It was becoming an issue at work as she couldn't find the time to finish her projects or meet her deadlines; she wasn't attending meetings and didn't know how to handle the amount of work she had on. It seemed like the more she tried to fit everything in the less she achieved.

So, I asked her to run through a typical day in her life, and to be as specific as possible, to see if we could sort out a new schedule together to address her time management problem. This is a summary of what she told me:

'I get up at 5am and weigh myself. Then I jog three miles to the gym and take a spinning class which lasts an hour. Then I walk from the gym to work which takes about half an hour. I arrive at the office at 7am and start working. At lunchtime, I go to the office gym for an hour. I am busy all day until 9pm and then I leave and usually meet a friend or attend a late night showing at the local cinema. I go to bed around midnight and then the day begins again ...'

As you may imagine, I was getting a little suspicious about Lucy's original dilemma. From this description, it seemed like time management wasn't the extent of her problems. So, I casually asked her when she had time to fit in meals. She laughed and told me that she ate a mandarin at 10am every morning and had a 'proper lunch' of soup but sometimes didn't have time for dinner. 'In fact, last night,' she told me, making eye contact for the first time and leaning forward conspiratorially, 'I totally pigged out!' Apparently, Lucy had been at a work dinner and had eaten a small piece of fish. This was her version of binge eating.

Well, I won't go on about it, but the conversation soon turned to eating difficulties.

Lucy's story

Lucy (age 25) admitted she had been anorexic since she was a teen but hadn't really thought about seeking help until her boss had a go at her about her poor time management skills.

'My eating problem is taking over my life. I have no time for anything else. Every minute of the day is allocated to my condition. If a meeting clashes with the time I eat my fruit or my soup, then I don't attend. I hide in the bathroom or canteen and then make excuses when my boss asks me why I wasn't there. Anyway, sometimes, I don't even have time for lunch; nobody takes a lunch break in my department as we are too busy, and it would look bad if I was the only one that left my desk to go to the canteen and sit down for lunch.'

I have a boyfriend but he doesn't understand what I'm going through. At first, I lied to him about my problems with food. Whenever he invited me out for dinner I pretended I had already eaten or that I couldn't eat what was in front of me as I was a fussy eater. One night, out of the blue, he arrived at my door with lots of shopping and announced he was going to cook for me. I totally flipped out and it was then that he guessed I had a condition. He has stayed with me, though, but I find myself withdrawing from him more and more each day.

He begs me to eat and that makes me panic. I make plans to see him but I always break them because I can't seem to fit him in around my eating problem. We have been together for a couple of years and I love him, but there is no way I can move our relationship forward because I can't live with him; it would mean he would witness my condition and that horrifies me. It's bad enough that he watches me eat and asks what I've eaten each day!'

In excess

Eating disorders such as binge eating, anorexia and bulimia are characterized by a constant preoccupation with food, body weight, and appearance. Lucy was anorexic; in her case, it involved long periods of fasting followed by self-induced vomiting or the taking of laxatives almost immediately after food was consumed. Anorexia can also take another form: binge eating and then purging afterwards; in fact, it is common for bulimia sufferers to have had anorexia prior to bulimia.

Typically, eating disorders such as binge eating, anorexia, and bulimia can be characterized by the following:

- Fear of losing control around food and weight gain
- Refusal or difficulty to adhere to the normal weight for age and height
- Fluctuating weight
- Obsession with the amount of fat/calories in food
- Fear of eating around others
- Denial that they have a weight problem or have a problem at all
- Hiding food
- Chronic dieting
- Mood swings, irritability, fatigue, depression, anxiety
- Poor sleeping habits

Physical effects of eating disorders include:

- Irritable Bowel Syndrome (IBS)
- Hair loss

- Bad teeth
- Feeling faint or dizzy
- Osteoporosis
- Damage to heart and kidneys
- Damage to throat

In our weight-obsessed culture, it is understandable that many of us will try and achieve that unattainable goal of beauty: the perfect body. However, there is a difference between dieting and an eating disorder. Most of us have been on a diet at one stage or another, or at least known someone who has. The majority of us will have been 'guilty' of binge eating especially at the weekend, when we feel we deserve it after a hard week at work. However, whilst we may have fleeting moments of remorse over the amount we drink or eat, we will not become obsessed by it, but put it behind us and, perhaps, try and not repeat the same behaviours too often.

Filling the gap

Binge eating is also becoming more and more common in our society. One patient of mine, John, an accountant in a City law firm, would binge-eat in secret.

John's story

For fear of being recognized, John would go to different shops during his lunch break, and buy huge quantities of sweets and chocolate. Sometimes the compulsion to eat was too much and he would eat the sweets and have to pay for the empty wrappers at the cashier's till. He also noticed that he entered a 'trance-like' state when he was eating a large amount of food; during this stupor, he would be completely unaware of how much he was consuming until he snapped out of it and saw all the leftover wrappers and packaging.

As John was overweight, he was subjected to a lot of comments from others at work that called him lazy and told him he lacked self-discipline. This exacerbated the way John thought about himself and made him feel like a failure. He refused to eat in front of his work colleagues at lunchtime for fear they would tease him further about his weight. However, not eating left him feeling even hungrier which led to him to binge even more when he was on his own. The only way he felt better was when he ate, but he would despise himself after a bingeing session. John then tried to diet, depriving himself of all the 'bad' foods. However, this only served as a temporary measure and whenever he 'broke' his diet, he would feel like a failure all over again.

One day, John was feeling very low and felt the urge to binge. As he was due to take part in a conference call, he didn't feel he could leave work to buy food so he was forced to go to the office canteen. However, by the time he got there, it was closed. John was caught by one of the kitchen staff raiding the fridge. His boss was told and they advised him to seek help.

Fearing the worst

What many people don't understand is that eating disorders have very little with to do with physical hunger, being lazy, or lacking self-discipline. They are a way of dealing with uncomfortable emotional feelings. Eating or not eating, exercising excessively or purging may be a way of relieving anxiety or other low and distressing feelings.

Because we haven't learned more helpful ways to deal with disturbing emotional feelings, we deal with them physically, through food, body appearance and weight control. It is about a fear of losing control: a fear of uncomfortable feelings in relation to our perceived failings, inadequacy, and social rejection.

As Lucy mentioned: 'I have no control over my external environment, and I can't seem to manage or communicate my feelings. Purging makes me feel in control of something: my own body.' Of course, dealing with our feelings in this way is extremely dangerous and can lead to depression, anxiety, and isolation.

Diving deep

Neither John nor Lucy developed eating disorders just because they were called names or told off at work; these situations simply triggered very painful underlying and unresolved emotional feelings in relation to their self-perceived level of competency and social acceptability: their self-worth. The following is Lucy's account of her past:

'When I was young my parents gave us all labels. I was known as 'the chubby one'. My sister was 'the pretty one' and my brother was 'the clever one'. They were all supposed to be affectionate nicknames and mine didn't bother me until I got a bit older. One day, when I was about 15, one of my friends went up to a lad I fancied at school and told him that I was mad about him. She reported back to me that he told her that I was a nice girl but a bit too 'fat' for him. I was absolutely gutted and hated myself for my big tummy and boobs. It was then I started fasting; starving myself and vomiting anything I ate. I told myself that if only I was a bit thinner, this boy would fancy me.

Over the course of a few months, my family began to notice my weight loss. I can remember feeling completely triumphant when my dad looked at me one day and said: 'Look how slim you are becoming, Lucy; we will have to find a new nickname for you soon!' It was one of the happiest moments of my life. But it wasn't enough to be a bit slimmer; I had to be the thinnest girl in school. In fact, I had to be the best at everything. Anything less than perfection was absolutely unacceptable to me.

I set up a silent competition with my friends, setting myself targets to lose enough weight to be thinner than them. Whenever I met my goals, I would feel a brief moment of joy but then would set the bar even higher to lose even more weight. Suddenly, I became the 'thin one' to the envy of my pals. I never got together with that boy I fancied. Somehow it didn't seem important any more. What was important was my food intake and how it affected my weight.'

Pointing the finger

There are no proven reasons about whom or what is to 'blame' for eating disorders in families. In some cases, eating disorders run in the family, but they might also be a result of feeling unrecognized and unconsidered. They may also be a response to over-critical parents or siblings or even mental/sexual abuse. For example, John came from a very successful family and felt pressured to 'toe the line' and make a name for himself. He felt he was unfairly criticized and humiliated by his parents when he didn't get full marks in his accountancy exams. This led him to comfort eat which, in turn, started to escalate out of control.

However, irrespective of the significant and triggering past events, it is fundamentally important to get to the root of the problem in the present and address those unbearable feelings of low self-esteem in order to begin the recovery process. The following diagram illustrates the link between low self-esteem and eating problems.

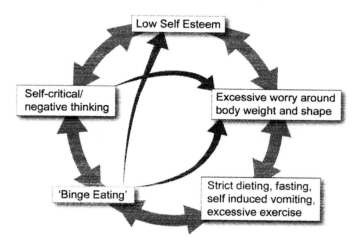

Figure 8. The vicious cycle of low self-esteem and eating problems.

It is important to recognize that food and weight control has become a way of solving what appear to be overwhelming problems, and the emotions related to them. It is important to ask yourself: 'Why do I have an urge to not eat now? Why do I feel the urge to overeat now? What is the problem that lies behind this feeling?'

Practice makes perfect

Again, those with eating disorders seem to fall prey to perfectionism. Setting high expectations for ourselves isn't a bad thing; we all need goals and something to strive for. But perfectionists want to achieve perfection in an area of their lives at any cost. Those with eating disorders tend to punish themselves if they 'fail' or fall short of their expectations or the expectations of others. They then lose confidence and self-esteem, thinking to themselves: I'm useless. I will never get that promotion if I'm not perfect in my work. Others will think I'm lazy and careless if I put on weight.

When they are low or have experienced a stressful incident at work or otherwise, the only way they feel in control is by punishing themselves. For example, when Lucy set a goal to lose 10 pounds in a week but only lost 8 pounds, she starved herself for days in order to achieve her goal.

She would also work incredibly long hours, checking and double-checking her work over and over again; making sure it was perfect. Of course, working long hours and making sure she was occupied outside work was another way of distracting her from eating or think-ing about food; therefore she felt completely in control of herself.

All or nothing

With eating problems comes all or nothing thinking. People see eve-rything in black and white: I am either a success or a failure. There is no 'in-between'. In John's case this would mean: 'I have just broken my diet and had a piece of chocolate. I might as well have the whole bar, and everything else, as I have failed anyway and there is no coming back.'

Challenging 'all or nothing' thinking is an important step towards recovery. Just because you feel you have fallen off the wagon doesn't mean your situation is hopeless. If you saw somebody that was sup-posed to be on a diet, eating a doughnut, you wouldn't automati-cally think: They're never going to lose weight now; that's it; it's all over for them. If you had any thoughts at all about it, you would probably think that they had a slip up and would return to their normal eating patterns the next day etc. However, the chances are you wouldn't think anything of it.

Heads up

The first step to recovery is to tell a trusted friend, family member (they will probably have guessed already) or a counsellor if it makes you feel more comfortable. This can be difficult as eating disorders are associated with secretive behaviour, thus, you may have isolated yourself to such an extent that you have lost contact and communi-cation with others. However, it is vital that somebody else is aware of your condition.

Much as you may wish to avoid it, it is probably wise to confide in a work colleague or your boss. Simultaneously, working and having an eating disorder is almost impossible and it is important that somebody in work knows that your disappearances and lack of attention aren't down to a lack of interest, or laziness.

However, many people with eating disorders keep their behaviour a secret, especially in work, as they feel there is a stigma about mental illness. They are afraid that others will think them weak, inadequate, out of control, unreliable and untrustworthy; characteristics that are totally unacceptable in the corporate world. Many feel that by broadcasting their condition they will be rejected by their colleagues and maybe lose their job as a result.

But confiding in someone also brings about tremendous relief. It is a great feeling to know that you have a friend you can trust; someone you can call when you are going through a rough patch.

Breaking out

Sufferers of eating disorders tend to have a rigid daily routine, so much so, that there is no room left for anything else. Lucy absolutely had to have her piece of fruit at 10am every day. When I suggested she eat at a different time in order to attend work meetings etc., she was absolutely horrified. She was afraid that if she didn't, she would be even more hungry, lose control, and eat more food, which would be catastrophic for her. Then I asked her why she didn't eat at her desk. She told me that she couldn't eat in front of others for fear they would be watching her and judging her.

Rituals are extremely important for those with eating disorders as they make them feel they are in control. When they meet each goal they set themselves during the day, they feel happy with themselves for mentally ticking off each item on the list:

- Two hours at the gym—check
- Desired food intake—check
- Weight goal—check

Of course, if something on the list isn't ticked off and they miss a gym session or eat something 'bad', then disaster strikes: negative thoughts set in (I am useless, disgusting, fat etc.) and a punishing behaviour begins (excessive exercise, fasting, vomiting, taking laxatives). Purging is accompanied by a temporary sense of relief but this is usually followed by feelings of despair, depression and anxiety (I can't believe I just did that to myself. Why can't I stop?).

So, how do you break the cycle? Getting thought and food diaries together is a really useful way of looking at your daily habits and examining the reasons behind those rituals. In other words, it is important that the feelings buried in your subconscious are made conscious in order to find the patterns of behaviour, thoughts and feelings that are associated with maintaining your eating disorder.

Diaries allow us to become more self-aware. For example, when Lucy wrote down her daily routine, she was surprised to find that she spent very little time at home, and exercised a lot each day. This prompted her to try and have an evening in at least once a week, and to do less exercise.

The following is an extract from Lucy's food diary:

Food / Drink	Feelings	Situation / Trigger / Thoughts	Compensatory Behaviour	Feelings / Thoughts after
Salad with salad dressing	Anxiety	At work lunch. "How can I get out of this? There's nothing on the menu that I can eat. I will have to eat or they'll think I'm weird!"	Vomited in toilet	Anger, disgust despair. "I hate myself, why can't I stop vomiting?"
Black coffee with sugar	Anxiety, guilt	At home leaving for work. "It's such a busy day; how will I get to the gym at lunch time? I shouldn't have had that sugar!"	Ran up the escalators and ran to work from the station	Relief and happiness. "I better not eat for the rest of the day to make sure I get rid of that sugar".

By monitoring food intake and challenging the thoughts and feelings that are the foundation of compensatory and punishing behaviours, Lucy was able to understand her condition and the 'triggers' that led to an episode. For example, she could challenge those negative thoughts about whether she really believed that she needed to not eat for the rest of the day. Once she broke down the reasons behind her reactions, she was able to think about the situation more rationally and adjust her habitual behaviours.

She was also able to rationalize her thinking around jumping to conclusions about what others were thinking. For example, maybe her work colleague wouldn't think she was weird not eating, just not that hungry, and pleased that she was to be joining them anyway.

Similarly, John was able to analyse his bingeing behaviour triggers by writing down his thoughts before and after an eating session; he was then able to understand the reasons behind his behaviour and ways in which he could address the thoughts and low feelings that fuelled it.

Over time, and with professional help, Lucy was also gradually able to increase the intake of food back into her diet by writing and attempting to stick to a food plan each day. This included certain foods that she had previously avoided because of their 'calorific' content. She wrote a hierarchical list of the foods that she had been avoiding and attempted to introduce the less 'scary' ones first.

It was important for her to regain some balance in her diet in terms of the foods she ate and the regularity in which she had her meals. In time, she was able to do this without feeling the need to purge or take laxatives.

John also wrote and stuck to a food plan which looked like this:

Wednesday

Time	Meal	Food / Drink
7.45am	Breakfast	Muesli and two slices of toast, coffee
10.15am	Snack	Banana and a coffee
1.15pm	Lunch	Vegetable soup, two slices of bread, low fat spread, low fat yogurt
4.30pm	Snack	Cup of tea
7.45pm	Dinner	Grilled chicken, green beans and baked potato, low fat chocolate mousse
10.30pm	Snack	Cup of tea and two biscuits

John was, understandably, a little concerned and anxious, at first, as his plan seemed to include eating many times throughout the day. Previously, he had tried to eat less and less often in his attempt to lose weight and he was concerned what others at work would think if they saw him snacking throughout the day.

However, he began to understand how eating regularly was an effective way to prevent binge eating, as the times between planned eating were short. If he felt hungry at times when he was not scheduled to eat then he could encourage himself to wait a short while until he had his next planned meal or snack. John realized that he had to devise a slightly different plan at the weekends when he would need to attend to other activities than his work. However, he tried his best to stick to the food plan.

Before going to the supermarket, John would also write a list of what he needed rather than haphazardly throwing goods into his trolley; he also tried to avoid shopping when he felt hungry. He limited the amount of 'bingeable' food in his home and always ate from a plate at the table, rather than hiding away in his room.

Soon, John began to realize that fasting, dieting, and depriving himself of certain foods just increased his physical and emotional desire to 'binge'. Taking the more gradual approach of eating 'little and often' helped John feel he was more in control of his eating habits.

Fight the power

Typically, those with eating disorders have trouble communicating their feelings to others. In Lucy's case, she was too afraid to talk to her parents about how being called 'the chubby one' hurt her feelings. Her family wasn't big on confrontation and she was afraid if she said something, she would be laughed at and dismissed as being overly sensitive and teased even further.

However, when she developed an eating disorder, she was no longer subjected to name-calling and this made her feel great, as if she had won the respect of her parents by losing weight. As she became more ill, she enjoyed the attention from her family and no longer felt invisible. She also felt satisfaction within herself that she had the willpower not to eat and felt strong because she was able to control her food intake.

This may sound like there are some advantages to having an eating disorder and these are the very reasons that people struggle to let go.

They fear that without their condition and the sense of control it brings; they will lose the love and attention they are receiving from friends, family and/or work colleagues, which means they won't be in control anymore. This is why it is so important to work through the physical, social and emotional reasons behind the disorder:

So, write down a list of advantages to keeping your eating 'problem' alive and ask yourself: What are you getting out of it? Why are you doing it? How does it make you feel better?

In the next column, write down a list of disadvantages and ask yourself: How does it make you feel bad? What are the things in life you are missing out on by having an eating disorder? When do you wish you didn't have it?

This is an example of Lucy's chart:

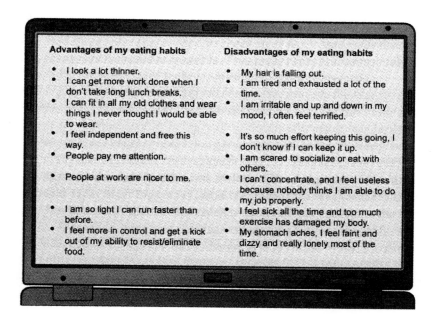

Advantages of my eating habits	Disadvantages of my eating habits
• I look a lot thinner.	• My hair is falling out.
• I can get more work done when I don't take long lunch breaks.	• I am tired and exhausted a lot of the time.
• I can fit in all my old clothes and wear things I never thought I would be able to wear.	• I am irritable and up and down in my mood, I often feel terrified.
• I feel independent and free this way.	• It's so much effort keeping this going, I don't know if I can keep it up.
• People pay me attention.	• I am scared to socialize or eat with others.
• People at work are nicer to me.	• I can't concentrate, and I feel useless because nobody thinks I am able to do my job properly.
• I am so light I can run faster than before.	• I feel sick all the time and too much exercise has damaged my body.
• I feel more in control and get a kick out of my ability to resist/eliminate food.	• My stomach aches, I feel faint and dizzy and really lonely most of the time.

Now, compare your list and think about the areas you would like to improve. You have two choices: to free yourself of your eating problem or to stay where you are. This list will, hopefully, put you into a better position to make that decision.

It sounds clichéd but an eating disorder can sometimes be a cry for help. It is a way of silently screaming that you need attention, but when you get it; it's often not the right sort of attention. We are looking for a certain type of support—understanding and empathy. However, sometimes we get the opposite—rejection.

Lucy experienced rejection when those around her didn't seem to understand what she was going through. They would tell her to 'try and eat a bit more', which didn't help her feel understood at all. Similarly, John did not find certain comments helpful or when others seemed to minimize his problem, by saying: 'try to go on a diet and do some exercise, it's easy if you put your mind to it!' Other people may mean well with such comments but they don't help to address the underlying feelings of incompetency, inadequacy, or rejection that both Lucy and John feel inside.

Hiding away

At first, there are initial feelings of euphoria associated with significant weight loss. People notice you, they compliment you and, in some cases, start to envy you. However, as the condition takes hold, you end up isolating yourself from others for fear they will discover your secret or not understand; if people think you aren't as perfect as you make out, they might criticize or judge you and that would be too painful to bear.

Those with eating disorders tend to end up isolating themselves from others. So many aspects of our social lives are down to food: work dinners, lunch with friends etc. For example, Lucy was too afraid to socialize for fear she would lose control, give into temptation and eat something.

A gradual return to socialising is the best way to get yourself back out there. Make an effort to go along to a work gathering; you don't have to stay for the entire night nor do you have to be the life and soul of the party. Just attending, and staying for a little while, over time, will help to build up your confidence and self-esteem.

Pushing back

As we have seen, those suffering from eating disorders connect self-worth with their body weight. When I asked Lucy how she would describe herself if she didn't have an eating disorder, she was lost for words. When the condition takes hold, it can colour every single aspect of your life; and it gets to the point where it defines you. Your self-worth and reason for being is influenced, connected, or motivated by your condition.

Living the dream

Picture yourself free of your condition and ask yourself the following:

- What would you like to be? Are you happy in your current job or do you think you would like to do something else for a living? Can you see yourself working there for another ten years?
- How would you like to be? Do you want to be happy, go out with friends, have better relationships with family, work colleagues etc.?
- What do you want out of life? Marriage? Husband? Children? A new house?

These may seem like impossible achievements right now, but visualising yourself without your eating disorder will help you realize how much you are, and will be, missing out on in life if you don't try to take steps to overcome it.

Setting goals

Gently setting achievable goals is a great way of separating yourself from your eating disorder. When you realize you can gain instant satisfaction through other means, it will give you the confidence to know that there are other ways to boost self-worth and feel good without damaging yourself. Creating a new daily routine is a good way of setting achievable goals. Lucy's old routine was absolutely exhausting.

When I suggested that she try and exercise less she responded with a valid point: 'Exercise is good for you, surely you're not asking me to stop that?' I asked her to rethink her reasons for the amount of exercise that she did. Was it to improve her general fitness, concentration and de-stress or was it more about weight loss and control? She confirmed the latter. The thing is that most things done in excess are not that good for us, including exercising. It's about finding a healthy balance.

Together, we devised simple methods to make her life a little less hectic, for example, getting the bus to the gym instead of walking three miles; only exercising once or twice a week instead of every day; and standing on the escalators in the Tube stations rather than running up them. They sound like simple changes but by replacing some of the more strenuous activities with alternatives, it helped to distract her from her old habits and focus her attention on other areas. She soon began to realize that by exercising less she did not suddenly balloon with weight, and she found that she could feel great about herself in other ways without strictly controlling her weight.

As Lucy was at the beginning of her recovery, we set the following goals together to gradually put her on the right track:

- Limit dieting and try and introduce one more ingredient/food that you usually avoid and larger portions into your diet each week, for example: full fat mayonnaise rather than low fat or butter on your toast rather than low fat margarine, and two slices of bread rather than one with your soup at lunchtime.
- If you feel you have overeaten, remember that although your stomach may be physically bloated it does not mean you have put on weight; it will pass.
- Try not to view bingeing or purging as 'failures' or 'relapses'; they are 'learning experiences' and without them you will not be able to learn ways to overcome your condition.
- Weigh yourself twice a week instead of twice a day.
- Try not to judge your weight by the way your clothes fit you.
- Try and avoid studying yourself in the mirror:
  (If you do look in the mirror balance every negative thought that you have about yourself with a positive one. For example, I hate the loose skin on my stomach but look how great my hair is today!)
- Take every opportunity to try and challenge your belief that body appearance and weight relate to your self-worth. Ask yourself what other qualities or behaviours do you have that are admirable, attractive, and worthy outside of the way you look.
- Attempt to spend at least one evening at home per week.
- Set half-an-hour aside each day to monitor your feelings and check in with how you are coping. Be aware that feelings pass; so if you are feeling low; accept you are feeling sad but also find comfort in the fact that these feelings will pass.
- Avoid pro-anorexia websites and other media that promote eating disorders and only value people by the way they look.

- Replace your usual habits with other enjoyable distractions that preferably have nothing to do with food or heavy exercise, for example: new hobbies, reading, chatting to friends, having a bath, taking a walk etc.
- If you are feeling stressed and have a compulsive need to purge, try and vent your emotion through other means such as screaming into a pillow, taking a walk, reading a book, listening to a relaxation CD, talking to a friend or therapist, or writing a letter to the person that upset you, but not sending it!
- If work is stressing you out, then duck out of the office for a short while to gather your thoughts and calm yourself down.
- Eat slowly, sitting down away from the kitchen, and not in front of the TV if you can help it!

Clangers: Friends and family

Eating disorders are very difficult for others to understand and despite all their good intentions it is likely they will get impatient, frustrated, and angry with the sufferer. So here are some tips about what not to say to someone with an eating disorder:

- What you need is a good roast dinner, that'll sort you out.
- If you want to lose weight, just eat healthily and do a bit of exercise.
- Have you put on weight?
- Men don't like really thin/fat women.
- Let's all get together as a family and have a big dinner.
- None of your family ever had an eating disorder. Where did yours come from?
- In some countries, people are dying of starvation, how could you be so ungrateful?
- You're just looking for attention; there's nothing wrong with you. Now, finish your dinner and stop being so ridiculous.

The statements above come from those that do not understand the complex nature of eating disorders. It is extremely helpful if a loved one accompanies the sufferer to counselling/therapy sessions in order to understand more about the condition and how they can provide the best help and support possible during the recovery.

Never say never again

Saying that you will never relapse or fall prey to your eating disorder again is another form of black and white thinking, again, putting yourself under far too much pressure. Life is all about ups and downs and you may experience some changes that you find stressful or traumatising: moving house, losing a loved one, being made redundant etc. It is tempting to look for the familiar during these times of change and that's when you may return to your old habits. However, if you do, then it doesn't mean you will never get better.

If you relapse, even after months of treatment, don't be too hard on yourself. You must try to forgive yourself for setbacks. Try and ask yourself: What else can I learn from this experience to help me overcome my condition? Remember: episodes of repeating old habits are not 'failures'; they are 'learning experiences'! Besides, if you have been undergoing therapy, it is more likely you will have the tools to pick yourself up, dust yourself off and continue along the road to recovery.

The upshot

Breaking any habit can be a long and very gradual process. However, recovering from an eating disorder is entirely possible; there is no reason why you can't kick the habit for good. By accepting that recovery isn't going to happen overnight, setting realistic goals, and forgiving yourself for any setbacks, you will find that each day becomes a little easier.

CHAPTER SEVEN

The phantom menace

"It is far more difficult to murder a phantom than a reality."
—Virginia Woolf

Managing pain is always tricky, but dealing with pain that, medically, shouldn't even exist, is even worse. You may hear this sort of pain described as somatic or phantom pain, but before I go any further, I want to make one thing perfectly clear: the pain is real. It may go undiagnosed by the medical field, but this does not mean the pain does not exist. Therefore, somatic complaints are not to be merely dismissed as 'all in your head', the physical pain is very real.

There is a common assumption out there that somatic complaints such as Chronic Pain and Chronic Fatigue, are strictly reserved for middle-class housewives who have ironed one shirt too many. However, Chronic Pain can affect anybody irrespective of their social class or profession. Indeed, a large majority of my patients who work in highly pressurized jobs in City suffer from these complaints.

So, what is Chronic Pain?

Chronic Pain is characterized by recurring and, sometimes, undiagnosed physical complaints that may last for long periods (usually more than six months). These pains may come in the form of headaches, feelings of lethargy, or other bodily aches and pains. Often, the pain is triggered by some sort of trauma to the body such as a viral infection, an operation, or an injury to bones or joints. Even after the infection or injury has healed, the sufferer may still feel the physical symptoms of their illness which can become very debilitating over time.

For the purpose of this chapter, the following fall under the category of Chronic Pain:

• Irritable Bowel Syndrome (IBS)
• Chronic Fatigue Syndrome (CFS)
• Backaches
• Headaches
• Joint pain

A note about IBS and CFS

IBS usually occurs after an infection or a series of stressful life events. It is characterized by mild to severe abdominal pain which can lead to diarrhoea, and constipation. There is no known cause and no proven cure for IBS so it is important to learn how to manage it. Worrying about it and allowing it to become the focal point of your life can lead to anxiety which, in turn, exacerbates the physical symptoms.

Again, there is no known cause for Chronic Fatigue, although like IBS it sometimes occurs following a viral illness; it is also thought to be a stress-related condition. It is characterized by: muscle or joint pain, poor sleep, low mood, headaches, dizziness, memory, and concentration problems. Those regarded as 'perfectionists' may suffer from CFS and IBS more than others.

David's story

David was a high flyer in the City, a keen sportsman, and was particularly keen on long-distance running. One day, he fell awkwardly and twisted his knee. He had an operation and was told to rest his knee for a week before making a return to work. Although David was in the middle of a crucial point in a work project, he reluctantly agreed.

When David attempted to go to the office the following week, he found he could barely stand on both legs; his knee didn't seem any better at all. He managed to hobble to work and battle through the day by gritting his teeth and taking lots of painkillers.

Over the next few weeks, David was still in a lot of pain and he made countless trips to his doctor, believing that something had gone wrong during the operation. Many more tests were carried out, but the doctors couldn't come up with any reason why David was still in so much pain. In fact, they told him that his knee was absolutely fine and there was no reason why it should still be hurting him.

David wasn't just struggling at work, but also at home. He had used running as a way of burning off frustration and because he couldn't run anymore, he was beginning to take his frustration and anxiety out on his wife, Deborah:

'Any time she tries to help me, I feel like screaming at her. I never used to be like this; I was always the capable one. I have always been good around the house, doing lots of DIY but because of my knee I am not able to do as much as I used to. If fact my pain seems to be spreading to my other knee and my lower back now—I can hardly do anything anymore. I'm afraid to do anything because the pain is so bad and I don't want to make it worse'.

As the months went on, David received no clear diagnosis for his condition. He was beginning to become demoralized, thinking that maybe it was all in his head; that there was nothing wrong with him at all:

'Sometimes I think I'm going crazy. I have lived with this pain for months and nobody can offer me a way out. Nobody seems to understand what I'm going through. Whenever I test out my knee, I feel a sharp pain but there is no reason for the pain. Pain-killers only have a short-term effect and the pain is taking over my ability to work the way I used to.

In work, I am having trouble managing my team. They seem sympathetic but they are probably thrilled that I am having difficulties as it means they don't have as much to do. It's so embarrassing that they see me hobble around like this! My boss has told me to take time off work but I am up for promotion and if I am not present, I will lose visibility and end up missing out, I'm sure.'

Eventually, David felt so distraught with his situation that he decided to seek alternative forms of therapy in an attempt to get to the root of his Chronic Pain.

After a couple of sessions with David, he told me that he had been to yet another doctor who suspected that there might be something medically wrong with his knee, after all, and wanted to run some more tests. Hugely relieved, he rushed in to tell me that he would probably not need my services any further; it looked like the pain wasn't all in his head; he wasn't going nuts!

David also told his boss that the doctors had finally admitted there may be something wrong with him and told him that he would keep him informed about the results of the tests.

The tests came back completely clear and David was devastated. With no medical diagnosis, he felt low, anxious, and frustrated; he felt completely hopeless about his future.

Jenny's story

Jenny was a consultant at a big accountancy firm in the City. She was knocked off her feet by a severe flu virus and ended up taking a couple of weeks off work. When she attempted a return to work, she struggled to make it through the day; her head felt fuzzy; she felt exhausted all the time, and she had trouble concentrating. She felt continually lethargic and her body seemed to ache all over.

When she went to pick up her kids, she felt she had to physically drag herself to the school gates and was unable to lift them up the way she used to. Months later, Jenny still felt that every day was a battle. She wasn't sleeping properly, and had terrible abdominal pains. She worried constantly about her lack of energy and what would happen if she couldn't make it through work the following day.

Jenny was suffering from CFS and IBS; she was continually exhausted and had intense diarrhoea as a result of her IBS which really affected her ability to function normally:

> 'I am tired all the time. When it's at its worst, I can barely get out of bed in the morning. Sometimes I can't even stand up. I should be able to get through this, what's wrong with me? I'll never feel active and happy again. I'm afraid to get on the Tube to work in case my IBS flares up. What if I don't get better? What will happen if I lose my job? I won't be able to support my children and then what will we do?'

The more Jenny thought about her condition, the more she aggravated her symptoms, but she couldn't help feeling hopeless about her situation. When I asked if she could maybe work from home a couple of days a week, she looked at me, completely horrified:

> 'Nobody works from home in my office; it's not that type of culture. The environment is very competitive; if they suspect something is wrong with me, they will find a way to get rid of me. It was bad enough taking off those initial two weeks! Anyway, if I take more time off, I may never be able to return to work; I have to keep myself going.'

Jenny continued to push herself to do everything she used to before, but every time she had a setback, she would lose confidence in herself:

> 'I used to be supermum—career woman and single mother all rolled into one. I was successful at my job and still found time to help the kids with their homework every night and drive them to all their sporting activities at weekends. I used to enjoy kicking a football around with my eldest son. Now I barely have the energy to pick up the car keys, never mind drive them anywhere.'

Like David, Jenny went to the doctor many times about how she was feeling. They gave her some pills to help with her IBS and told her she would get better, in time. Jenny felt that the doctor was merely humouring her and was just giving her pills to fob her off. Worried that she was going crazy, Jenny took a friend's advice to see a psychologist about her condition.

Pain management

As we mentioned previously, the pain is real. Both David and Jenny suffered from very real physical symptoms. The problem was they didn't know how to manage the 'pain'. Psychological therapy or medical treatment doesn't make it go away for good; it's about managing the distress associated with the pain. The more we worry the more adrenalin goes around our bodies, which can exacerbate hotspots of pain. (Please see Chapter Two for a diagram on the physical experience of worry and anxiety.) Furthermore, when we pay too much attention to it by continuing to check how bad it is, and worry and ruminate about it and how it is affecting our lives, we really only end up making the pain worse and become more distressed. Our level of activity by either doing too much or too little also exacerbates and affects our pain experience. People can find themselves in a vicious cycle of Chronic Pain and distress:

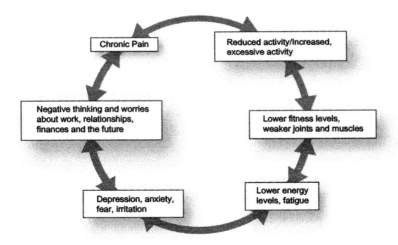

Figure 9. The vicious cycle of Chronic Pain.

So, it stands to reason that if we are less distressed about pain, we would have less physical symptoms and would, therefore, be able to deal with it better. Both David and Jenny experienced the same types of thoughts in relation to their conditions that fell into the following categories:

- Questioning their sanity.
- Frustrated with themselves as they are not the same as they used to be.
- Worrying about the future and where it all might end up.
- Angry when they do not receive a clear diagnosis, and with those that do not understand.
- Anxious about not getting enough sleep.

The pain affected every part of their lives: work, relationships, hobbies, activities etc. There is a tendency to feel totally hopeless about the situation and just give up. For example, because David was too afraid to start running again for fear of damaging his knee, he stopped exercising completely. As we shall see, challenging this 'all or nothing' thinking as well as other negative thoughts can make a big difference to the recovery process.

Watching your mouth

Using unhelpful thinking and language to approach your situation will make the experience even more difficult. For example, Jenny felt she *should* be supermum all the time and felt guilty if she wasn't constantly there for everyone else; whilst David thought he was *useless* and a *failure* for not being able to function the way he used to. He was *supposed* to be the strong one: the man who could do everything.

Using more helpful, alternative language can help you to better cope with your pain experience. Beating ourselves up only lowers our confidence further which exacerbates the situation as a result.

So, in Jenny's case, instead of focusing on what a terrible mother she was by not driving her kids to activities on the weekend, she began to use the following language:

'I wasn't able to bring the kids to football practise today but perhaps I will be able to go next weekend. If I still don't feel well enough then I will ask one of the other mothers to help me out. This is not how I would like things to be but I can accept this for now.'

Here, instead of beating herself up, she is more accepting of the problem and herself. She has 'eased-up' from her rigid way of thinking, and is offering herself an alternative. If that doesn't work then she will ask someone else to give her a hand. Although this alternative way of thinking does not entirely stop her from feeling frustrated, it does create a sense of relief and forward movement in her experience once again.

Similarly, David could try the same technique. Instead of telling himself he *should* be able to do everything at once at work, he could go easier on himself:

'Ok, so I lost concentration a bit in that meeting today but the chances are nobody noticed and I will just do my best to keep up in the next meeting.'

Acceptance is a crucial part to managing our Chronic Pain. This does not mean giving up or convincing ourselves that there is no pain or that we should just ignore or put up with the pain. It is about experiencing our pain and events as they are and not as we think they 'should' be. It is important to try to recognise that although your pain experience and circumstances may not be what you would like them to be, by accepting them for what they are and accepting the things that we cannot change, we can help regain a sense of control and a more hopeful outlook.

By challenging our self-critical and rigid thoughts, and realising what 'we can do' rather than all that 'we cannot do'; we can rebuild our shattered confidence and re-create a more optimistic sense of forward movement around a, seemingly, desperate situation.

Beating a dead horse

'Why me' is also a common reaction to Chronic Pain. As David says: 'Every time I leave the doctors without any clear indication of when I am going to feel better, I want to punch him. Why did this happen to me, of all people?'

Asking 'why' is a completely normal response whenever we experience an unpleasant and unexpected event. However, the anger and frustration that results from asking a question with no definite answer will only increase our distress and experience of pain (please see Chapter One for more information on 'Why?' questions).

Predicting the future is not something we are able to do, yet many of us try to second-guess what is in store for us by asking 'What if?' Certain events can trigger the pain and many of these are linked to worry and anxiety about the future.

Again, our thinking here is very important. David would lay awake at night plagued by 'What if' questions:

- What if I fail to make that promotion?
- What if my knee gets worse?
- What if my wife leaves me because I'm so weak?

The key to problem solving and to reduce the amount of worrying thoughts is to take each issue one by one and break it down. David started to write down his worries about certain problems, and tried to come up with helpful alternative thoughts and solutions to them as you can see below:

Problem	Makes me feel	Worry / Worst that could happen	Alternative viewpoint / Solution
Failure to get promotion	Terrified, anxious, panicky	I would stay in the same job for another year. Everybody would think I was useless.	I like my job and it wouldn't be so bad if I'm there another year. Maybe I could talk to my manager about it so he and I can set my expectations for the following year. My team respects me and they might feel sorry for me but they wouldn't think I was useless. I'll let them know that I will be working towards my promotion in time.

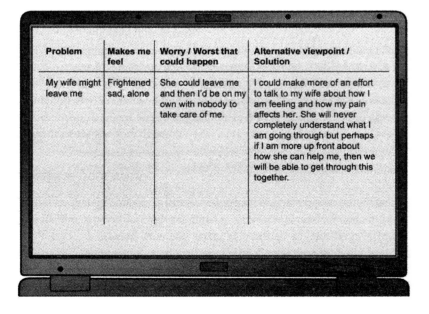

Problem	Makes me feel	Worry / Worst that could happen	Alternative viewpoint / Solution
Knee getting worse	Anxious, frustrated, depressed	I might never be able to run again	I may not be able to run as I did at the moment. But in the meantime, I could go to more physio sessions and do some light exercise, and maybe some swimming which I used to love, in order to be able to run again in the future.

Problem	Makes me feel	Worry / Worst that could happen	Alternative viewpoint / Solution
My wife might leave me	Frightened sad, alone	She could leave me and then I'd be on my own with nobody to take care of me.	I could make more of an effort to talk to my wife about how I am feeling and how my pain affects her. She will never completely understand what I am going through but perhaps if I am more up front about how she can help me, then we will be able to get through this together.

Writing down our thoughts is very helpful as it slows down our regretful rumination and catastrophic worrying and helps to settle our minds. It also allows us to understand how rumination and worry intensifies our low, frustrated, and anxious feelings and how these feelings affect our sleep and exacerbate our pain even more. Furthermore, this exercise helps us to focus on making some changes for the better. By challenging our negative thoughts and presenting alternative viewpoints, we can start to feel more confident and less helpless. It stands to reason that we tend to become more proactive in tackling the problems themselves, when we focus on what we *can* do rather than what we can't.

Barking up the wrong tree

When we get sick, we think we need to behave in a certain way: staying in bed, taking time off work, visiting a doctor, getting someone to look after us, and, generally, avoiding our usual routines until the illness passes. All these are sensible ways to approach recovery, as long as they are purely temporary measures. The following examines some of the myths we believe in when we aren't feeling well and looks at different ways to manage long-term pain.

Doctor, doctor!

It is understandable that most of us will seek medical advice and treatment when we experience some physical discomfort; of course this is most advisable. However, if we find ourselves seeking out opinion after opinion and our pain is still there it may be more sensible to stop this behaviour altogether. The worry and frustration that results from 'not getting anywhere' with medical advice and treatment will only exacerbate our 'pain' even more.

David came to realise that trying to find out the medical cause of his pain and attending physio session after physio session only frustrated him more and more as his pain did not seem to be getting any better. Despite it feeling scary and totally counterintuitive, David decided to stop looking for a medical cause to his pain and stopped attending physio altogether. He noticed how his mood and pain experience improved as a result.

Staying in bed

Most of us will take to bed when we are feeling under the weather. It is natural to rest if your body has experienced some sort of trauma such as an injury or viral infection. However, complete bed rest for longer than a couple of weeks can be quite harmful. If you are not being active, then your muscles and joints will cease up through lack of use, which will cause you even more pain. If this occurs, you might attribute this muscle or joint weakness to your original condition.

David became fearful of his pain so he avoided being active and didn't do as much activity and stretching as he used to. After some time, his muscles, ligaments, and tendons started to become short, stiff, and tight. Of course, this affected his movement which led him to assume that his pain was spreading over his body, and worsening. The diagram below helps to explain how our pain seems to spread from one body part to the next:

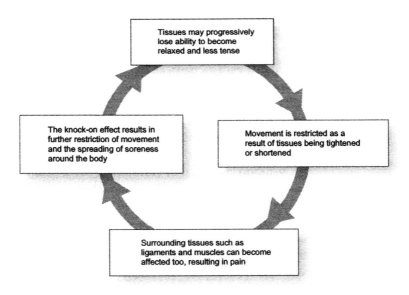

Figure 10. The experience of Chronic Pain spreading around our body.

Additionally, if we are inactive, we tend to notice the pain more. Keeping active is a way of distracting ourselves from the pain. Thus, being active is vital when battling Chronic Pain.

If we do less then we also might be missing out on opportunities for enjoyment and doing all the things that we still *can* do. For example: David used to go running with one of his mates every morning before work. When he hurt his knee, he stopped seeing his friend altogether which made him feel lonely and depressed.

Retreating into ourselves and avoiding things that we think we 'can't' or 'shouldn't' be doing, ends up making us feel stuck. Enjoying life becomes more threatening, as we risk our happiness being taken away from us by our condition. So, we would rather hide away then face possible disappointment by engaging in activities we would have enjoyed in the past. The trick is to keep doing the activities you used to, albeit at a slower pace or in a different way, and to try and find new activities that you still can do, all the time trying to focus your thoughts and attention on what you can do rather than what you can't.

Getting right back on that horse!

Of course, there are those of us that will want to get 'back to normal' as quickly as possible after an illness or injury. For example, Jenny continued to push herself in the same way as she did before she became ill. However, by trying to maintain the same high standards, she suffered more when she had a setback. Driving ourselves too hard sets us up for failure if we don't achieve our goals. Remember: our health usually suffers because of our lifestyles; the food we eat; the hours we work; and the general craziness of daily life. When we are overdoing it, our body tells us, 'Enough!' Rather than jumping back on that horse again, we need to let our bodies recover fully.

Suffering from ill health is a sign for us to make some changes in the way we live; whether it is diet-related, anxiety-related, or both.

Numbing the pain

When we are in pain, the first thing we reach for is some tablets to dull the uncomfortable feeling. However, there is no known treatment specifically for Chronic Pain, and whilst some painkillers might help in the short term, they will only provide temporary relief. Anti depressants can help alleviate the feelings of worry and anxiety but won't cure the pain itself. Therefore, it is far more important to take a look at how you're managing the pain rather than popping a few pills.

It's all in the family

Many people think that if they have a bad back or suffer from certain health conditions that they are bound to get it as it runs in the family. Contrary to what you might think, there are very few health conditions that are genetic. David's grandfather had a dodgy knee so he accepted that he contracted 'weak knees' from him. However, thinking like that doesn't help matters as it might prompt you to admit defeat: 'My mother had IBS so therefore I'm always going to have it. I can't do anything to make it better.'

Keeping an eye on it

Of course, it is prudent to look after yourself but constantly checking to see if the pain is there will only make it hurt more. Think about it: if one of your friends said to you, 'How's the knee today?' you would automatically focus on that particular body area. You might have been having a good day and had not given your knee too much thought at all, but now because it has been brought your attention, you check in with yourself and might feel that there is pain after all.

David would regularly check how his knee was doing, and even put pressure on his knee to the point where he felt pain. When he felt it intensely, he would be relieved as he would know the pain was real, and he was not going nuts. When he was most frustrated, he would deliberately go even harder on his knee to prove to himself and the doctor that his knee needed another operation. If David had a good day, he would take it to mean that the pain was all in his head, but if he felt agonising pain, paradoxically, he would feel better within himself as he could prove that it wasn't imaginary.

Thus, constant pain checking is unhelpful as it will seem like the pain is worse every time you monitor it. Remember: when you look for the pain the chances are you will find it!

Head in the sand

If you are in pain, do seek medical advice. Of course, not all long term pain is somatic, so it's important that you go and find out what is causing the discomfort; at least then you can do something about it. Although many people out there will go and see a doctor immediately if they feel pain, there are a good few of us who are afraid that something more sinister is causing the pain. For example, Jenny did not seek medical help for weeks after developing IBS as she was too embarrassed to tell the doctor about her diarrhoea. Also she was worried that if it was something more serious she would be signed off from work, and feared letting her team down or being seen as weak. When she found out, she was very relieved that it wasn't something more serious, thus knowing what it was enabled her to do something about it.

Getting your arms around it

When we are in pain, we tend to communicate it to those around us by doing the following:

- Crying
- Grimacing
- Moaning
- Complaining
- Limping

Those around us respond with sympathy to these pain noises and pain behaviours. However, if we are in pain, we don't necessarily want nor need constant reassurance and sympathy. For example, it drove David mad in work when one of his colleagues told him: 'You poor thing; having a knee injury is awful. Don't worry, you will feel better soon. My cousin had the exact same thing and he is fine now; he just ran the London Marathon actually ...'

When we are in pain, we are not looking for solutions, we are looking for empathy. David used to get so frustrated when his wife tried to do the DIY as he felt his position was being usurped. Deep down, he knew she was only trying to do him a favour but he couldn't help shouting at her. Of course, she would become confused and upset.

This made him feel terrible for acting that way towards her which lowered his mood and exacerbated his pain.

On another occasion, his wife took over washing the car when he hurt his knee:

> 'This annoyed me beyond belief. Firstly, this was always my job, and secondly, it's not like I'm a complete invalid. As time went on and she continued to wash the car every weekend, I just thought, let her. Maybe she's right; maybe I can't do it anymore. So now I just do nothing and she does everything.'

David has become bitter about his wife taking over and now feels isolated and withdrawn from her. He has lost the confidence in his own ability to do things for himself. Worst of all, he has no idea how to talk to her about it.

Working through the pain

Jenny tried to hide her discomfort and pain experience at work, and would put on a brave face so others would not be aware of what she was experiencing. She didn't want to be seen as weak or unable to manage, and didn't want to burden her colleagues with her distress.

This is fairly typical behaviour of people who suffer from pain. They don't want to talk about pain when they are in good form i.e., if they are enjoying a pain-free day, then they don't want to 'jinx' it by talking about it nor will they appreciate others bringing it up. Because they don't talk about their pain, people simply don't notice when they are in pain and will treat them as if they are a fully-functioning person. Thus, the person in pain feels others have very high expectations of them. However, unless they open up and talk about it then others will not know any better.

Therefore, it is important to talk to your partner and work colleagues about how you are feeling. We all have a tendency to mind-read what others are thinking instead of talking to them directly. Include your loved ones and colleagues in how you are feeling and what you would like to achieve. They can then help and support you towards meeting your goals.

Learning to successfully communicate with those around us is crucial to maintain relationships and to help manage our pain at home or at work. Confiding in someone can bring about tremendous relief and knowing that you have support is essential during your recovery.

The other side

It is not easy to live with somebody who is dealing with Chronic Pain. No matter how sympathetic you think you are being, there are certain types of phrases that you would be better off avoiding:

> 'Don't worry, you will feel better soon.'
> 'You shouldn't be doing that; here, let me.'
> 'You look wrecked today.'
> 'The doctor said there's nothing wrong with you. Stop moaning!'
> 'It's all in your head.'

Of course, you mean well, but your loved one or colleague is not going to thank you for using the above statements; in fact, it is more likely that you will get your head bitten off! What sufferers are looking for is understanding. A statement such as: 'I understand that you must be going through a lot of pain at the moment,' is a million times more effective than saying, 'Pull yourself together and stop whinging!' It is important that the sufferer knows that they are not alone in dealing with their pain, and that you at least try to understand from their perspective what they are going through.

Loss of confidence is also one of the first things to occur when coping with Chronic Pain. The more sufferers feel they are not getting any better, the more helpless and useless they will feel. Helping them out with certain tasks might be necessary in the short term but if you continue to do everything for them, they might engage in self-doubt and lose the confidence in their own ability to do certain things for themselves.

Similarly, if you do everything for your partner or colleague, they may lose their independence which leads to inactivity and low mood which, of course, gives them even more time to focus on their pain. If they suffer from Chronic Fatigue they may struggle to do 'simple' things like chop the vegetables, prepare the dinner, or photocopy a document. However, even if it takes them two hours to complete the task, it is important that you let them do it. For example: even if it took David all day to wash the car, he would be better off doing a task he wants to do rather than not doing it at all.

In short, as long as the sufferer is realistic about the tasks they want to carry out then it is important for you to encourage them and praise them for their achievements.

Getting your feet wet

The key to overcoming Chronic Pain is to pace yourself. Sufferers have a tendency to over do it on 'good days' and end up wiping themselves out for the rest of the week. Some people need to do more and some need to do less in order to regain balance. Often, doing too much worsens the problem, as in Jenny's case. For example, when Jenny had a 'good' day she did all the cooking and cleaning, and generally caught up on everything she had missed out on during her 'bad days'. She also tended to check in at work, and rush through as many work emails as possible. This meant that she completely over-did it and ended up feeling worse than ever afterwards.

The City is a demanding working environment. It is easy to fall into the trap of working all the time and feeling that we can't take a break at work; this way of being will undoubtedly affect our health after some time. We may work long hours, forget to eat properly, have too many late nights and end up getting lots of headaches and colds. CFS, in particular, is characterized by lots of flu symptoms. Of course, the cold virus itself triggers it but if we push ourselves too hard then we don't recover sufficiently, which only serves to exacerbate the virus.

When we have to take time off due to illness, the critic sets in: I should be at work, what will everybody think? What if I can't cope with the backlog when I return to work? The more guilty we feel for not being at work the more stressed we will feel. Thus, worry, anxiety, and frustration sustains the flu-like symptoms. This is how we maintain the illness, by living in a state of constant expectation: 'I *should* feel better by now.' 'I can't get rid of it.' 'The doctors *can't* find anything wrong with me.' 'I'm going crazy; it's all in my mind'. The more self-critical we become the more under-confident and helpless we feel. As we become more distressed with feeling low, angry, and frustrated, we further exacerbate our own pain condition.

Any quick fix is going to leave sufferers disappointed and will increase the problem. That's why pacing is so important. Family members, friends, and colleagues can play an important role by reminding you to pace yourself and to praise you for your achievements.

There are two fundamental areas to pacing:

- Taking lots of breaks
- Increasing activity at a gradual pace

Many of us will only take breaks if we are forced into it. If our shoulders and neck are tense because we have spent too long in front of the computer, only then will we take a break from the screen. However, planning breaks and making them an enjoyable experience helps us to avoid all those bodily aches and pains. For example, David wanted to be able to run long-distance again. Whilst he did not feel he could achieve this with his bad knee, he decided to try and build himself up to jogging for five minutes on a treadmill every other day. This involved doing a set amount of exercises per day which he would gradually increase as time went on. He planned plenty of breaks throughout the day, promising himself a cup of tea, or a ten-minute rest, listening to music, so he had something to look forward to.

When David completed his goal, he rewarded himself by contacting his running buddy and arranging to meet for lunch that weekend.

If you get the art of pacing right, you will feel more confident, have more energy, sleep better and your mood will be lifted. Most importantly, you will feel like you can achieve more. Gradually, you will find yourself doing tasks you never would have thought possible.

Moving the goal posts

Those of us who do not have Chronic Pain may not give it a second thought when it comes to achieving some of our goals or carrying out daily tasks. However, when we feel physical pain it may be important to focus on setting goals in a more structured way so we do not feel overwhelmed by the task.

So, if you're planning to build up to an event, it helps to set proper goals. These could be short, medium, or long term goals. Set daily or weekly targets, like going for a ten-minute walk every day. Take some time out to write down what you would like to achieve in the future. While you're doing that, write down how you would like to reward yourself before you even begin the task so you have something to look forward to when you have completed your goal. For example, Jenny wanted to attain a new accountancy qualification that she had never had time to do while she was working full time. She began to write down what she needed to do in order to apply for the course, breaking it down into smaller steps over a four-week period as you can see below. The reward she gave herself was a nice massage at her local spa once she had achieved her goal:

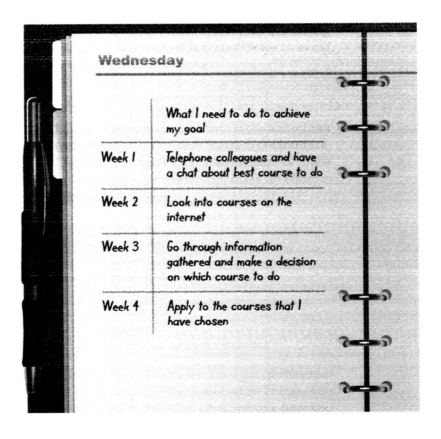

Wednesday

	What I need to do to achieve my goal
Week 1	Telephone colleagues and have a chat about best course to do
Week 2	Look into courses on the internet
Week 3	Go through information gathered and make a decision on which course to do
Week 4	Apply to the courses that I have chosen

By building herself up and setting smaller achievable and realistic goals, Jenny was able to achieve her, seemingly, impossible target of applying for an accountancy course.

Tips for dealing with Chronic Pain

Keep a pain diary

Sometimes we become so focused on the physical side of our experience that we forget how our behaviour, thoughts, and feelings are connected with our physical wellbeing. (Please see Chapter One for further explanation of how our thoughts, behaviour, and emotions are connected with our physical health.)

A pain diary is a helpful way of recording your levels of pain over a period of time at different times of the day. This gives you a better idea of the activities or situations, and unhelpful thinking patterns that trigger or worsen your pain. Identifying the pattern of your pain means that you can manage your pain better and helps you learn to avoid what actually triggers it. Below is an example of what a pain diary might look like:

Date	Time	Where is pain?	Rate the pain from 1 to 10	What were you doing when you felt the pain?

Once you complete your diary over a period of time, you will begin to understand more about your pain and plan your day accordingly.

Treat yourself to a massage!

Massages are great ways to alleviate the pain and relax those tired muscles. You could also use heat compresses or ice packs on the area, depending on the nature of the illness.

Distract yourself!

As ever, it is important to keep busy and do things that take your mind off the pain. (Please see Chapters Two and Four for more information on distraction techniques.)

Confront those situations!

If we are ill we tend to avoid those situations where we might feel uncomfortable or where we feel we are putting ourselves at risk. Jenny was particularly conscious of her IBS and worried constantly about being near a bathroom at all times. Therefore, she would avoid those places where there was not a toilet in close proximity.

To confront her fears, she drew up a list of difficult situations and rated them from 1 to 10 in terms of how anxious she felt about each one. As she looked at her list, she was able to devise a plan, using goal-setting techniques to challenge those situations she had been avoiding.

Relaxation and meditation!

Doing regular relaxation and meditation exercises, and learning to breathe properly will also help to control the pain (see Appendices I, II, and III). Make a list of all the ways you like to relax and do at least one of them everyday. These could include: a hot bath, listening to music, or reading a book.

Write it down

Whether you are goal setting, keeping a pain diary or devising your list of rewards, it is so important to write down how you are feeling.

If you have negative thoughts such as: I can't get out of bed or My knee is really bad today; then you can balance those statements with more helpful, alternative ones: I can get through this or If I keep myself busy I won't notice the pain as much.

Look after yourself!

It is important to eat healthily, drink lots of water, and to really make time for your meals. Avoid caffeine as it is a stimulant which increases anxiety symptoms which does not do your pain much good. Usually, when we get ill, it is our body's way of telling us we are run down, so make sure you look after it by eating well and doing regular exercise at a gradual pace.

Get some sleep

We will go into this in more depth in Chapter Nine but it is important to get a good night's sleep. Worry, anxiety, and lack of sleep will certainly exacerbate the pain. Sleeping during the day will affect your night-time sleep so try to avoid this, if possible. Try and also get up at the same time every day; this will help you to establish a healthy sleeping pattern.

Go easy on yourself

There will be times when you will suffer setbacks. Do not let this demoralize you; try to accept that it has happened and that it is an entirely understandable part of the process. Consider reducing activity and increasing the amount of relaxation exercises until you feel better again. During this period, it is important to think about how far you have come. Note down all your achievements over the previous few weeks and set new goals for when you are feeling better.

The upshot

Both David and Jenny arranged a phased return to work and organized lots of breaks during the periods they were at the office. They were brave to talk openly and honestly about their limitations to their managers and employers, and noticed the benefits of doing so. Although it can be difficult to admit you have a problem, you will usually find that most companies, and places of work, are a lot more understanding and supportive than you think. David and Jenny gradually overcame their conditions by learning to manage their pain. It took a few months off work and a couple of setbacks, but with the help of their colleagues, friends, and family, they noticed they were improving, little by little.

Because there is no clear cause or cure for Chronic Pain, it can be a very difficult and frustrating problem to deal with. Most of us would like to see some proof of our illness and when the diagnosis comes back inconclusive, we can feel a sense of hopelessness rather than relief. We may also be concerned about what others may think of us at work when we have no real diagnostic answer to give them. However, it is entirely possible to manage the pain by becoming more accepting of it, facing our fears of doing less (particularly with regards to work) and by looking after ourselves, physically and emotionally. By accepting that we need to change our lifestyles, we are able to ensure that we are operating to our fullest once more.

CHAPTER EIGHT

The weakest link

"The single biggest problem in communication is the illusion that it has taken place."

—George Bernard Shaw

P roductive communication is vital in any relationship, including those in our working environments. Without it, our relationships with others simply do not work or continue to feel unsatisfactory. Over the course of this book, we have looked at a number of mental health conditions such as eating disorders, depersonalization, anger management etc. Although these conditions may seem to be very different from each other, one thing they share in common is the potential to be very isolating.

Sometimes, we feel reluctant to communicate our feelings with others, particularly at work, when we are feeling down, depressed, or anxious. We are afraid that if we confide how we are feeling, we will look weak and go down in the estimation of our work colleagues. We may fear that others will see that we are not coping, and may worry about losing their respect, and potentially missing out on that bonus, or being the next one in line for the redundancy chop! This means that we end up hiding our feelings, retreating into ourselves, and isolating ourselves from others which makes things even worse.

Sharing our feelings is a vital step towards relieving our distress. However, it is *how* we communicate with others that makes the difference. There are many ways to communicate our feelings at work: sometimes we are passive, and at other times, we can be aggressive. As we shall see, neither of these behaviours will get us what we want.

Assertive communication is the best way towards having our needs met; however, many of us shy away from it by behaving passively, aggressively or even both at the same time! A passive or aggressive style of communication is an expression of the same thing: an underlying sense of low self-confidence. If you can strike the right balance between passive and aggressive behaviour, you will reach the point where it becomes assertive. However, some people remain passive because they fear if they are assertive they will be perceived as being aggressive. If they are aggressive, they fear it coming across as being passive. Thus there is that fear of going from one extreme to the other.

The following case study looks at the passive form of communication which is fully exemplified by Julie: 'the silent patient'.

Silence is golden ...

Every Monday at 6 pm on the dot, Julie would walk quietly into my office with her head bowed, and sit down with her ankles pressed neatly together; her hands clasped on her knee. Although I probably saw her more frequently than some of my own friends, I was still none the wiser about how to help her. This was because she said absolutely nothing for the entire session.

For months, she would walk in; shoulders slumped, and wring her hands for an hour, then get up and leave. I tried every tactic in the book to get her to open up but it soon became a teeth-pulling situation and I began to think that nothing would work. 'Easy money!' I hear you cry. Well, you might think so, but as a psychologist, there is nothing more frustrating than a patient that refuses to communicate. In a room filled with silence, ten seconds can feel like an hour.

Julie had been referred to me by her GP as she had been experiencing frequent panic attacks and couldn't bear them anymore.

The only other details I knew about her was that she was 32, single, and worked as a business analyst for a City firm.

Although I hate to admit it, I started to dread Julie's Monday visits. Every time the session ended, I felt even more frustrated and hopeless about my ability to help her. The more I pushed, the less she responded. I began to get tongue-tied and really struggled to come up with new ways to get her to open up. Because she refused to look at me, I had no way of gauging if I was getting anywhere. I was stuck.

As the weeks went by, I started to question why she even bothered turning up if she wasn't going to talk about her problem. In fact, I found myself becoming angry over the whole situation. Why didn't she feel she could talk to me? Was it something I was doing wrong? If so, why didn't she just go to someone else? I wondered how someone so uncommunicative could survive and succeed in the 'in-your-face' City working environment!

Then it hit me.

If I was feeling stuck, tongue-tied and helpless, perhaps, this was how she was feeling, too. Maybe she was struggling to find the right words in the same way I had been.

Usually, I am aware of how a patient feels by getting a sense of how I feel when I am with them. With Julie, it had just taken me a bit longer to get there.

So, the following Monday, I went in, determined to get something out of her. Fifty minutes of perseverance later, and still nothing. In desperation, I made an unbelievably poor joke, and the corner of her mouth twitched. She had just given me her first smile. Her hand immediately flew to her mouth to cover it, but it was too late, I had already seen her reaction. Encouraged, I pursued this line of humour and after a while, she raised her head and looked me in the eye. Major progress!

Over the next few sessions, she began, rather hesitantly, to open up. In a very soft voice, she started to tell me more about herself, and how she was feeling.

Julie's story

Julie had been having panic attacks for over ten years but they had become so bad that it had prompted her to go to the doctor. It turned out that her manager had made a general statement to her entire department that some of the staff were at risk of redundancy. Julie completely personalized this statement, thinking that her boss was sure to let her go. The thought of losing her job was so horrifying to her that she had been having massive panic attacks over it.

When I asked her if there was any reason why she would be targeted, in particular, she told me it was because nobody liked her in work and all thought she was useless. When I encouraged her to expand on this, she told me that nobody ever talked to her; they ignored her and walked all over her. She always had the toughest assignments and her boss gave her shorter deadlines than everyone else. I asked her why she didn't speak up about how she was feeling, but she said she didn't like confrontation and was afraid everybody would think she was stupid.

Her family history also told a story: she came from a conservative family that didn't allow expression of emotion or talking about personal matters. In the past, when she had tried to confront her parents about how she was feeling, she was told not to be so stupid, and then dismissed. As a result, she learned to associate expressing emotions with rejection, and she gradually retreated into herself. At school, she was an easy target because of her passive nature and her lack of ability to fight back.

All her life, Julie felt she wasn't good enough. When somebody sounded like they were angry with her, she would go to pieces, thinking she had been rejected. She would then go silent and bury all her anxious feelings in order to avoid any further confrontation. Eventually, her anxiety would manifest itself in panic attacks that left her drained and traumatized. Of course, her behaviour had a negative effect on all her relationships as she did not want to share with others how she was feeling, and didn't want to be seen as a burden. Additionally, she feared rejection if she confided in them. Julie was now in a position where she found herself completely isolated from everybody else.

Turtles at work

When we fail to express ourselves honestly and openly, there is a window of opportunity for others to walk all over us. Whilst the behaviour is a form of self-protection, allowing others to make decisions for us leaves us feeling helpless and powerless, and feeling like a doormat. Others pick up on non-assertive behaviour and tend to take advantage of our passive nature. They, too, may view our uncommunicative behaviour as a personal slight on them, and think the quiet person dislikes them. They may, therefore, stay out of their way which might heighten that sense of isolation for the passive person.

For example, Julie had booked a few days off from work; a work colleague had, subsequently, booked the same days. As only one person could leave the team at the same time, it meant that one of them had to cancel their holiday. Even though Julie had booked it first, she ended up cancelling it as she was afraid of what the other girl would think of her if she tried to defend herself. This left her feeling angry and resentful.

As with many passive people, Julie had a tendency to blame others for her misfortune:

> 'If only she was nicer to me then this wouldn't have happened'
> 'If my boss would just stop picking on me then I'd be much happier'

The problem with this way of thinking is that it puts the responsibility on others to behave differently towards us. In Julie's case, she was depending on her work colleagues to change, rather than taking charge of the situation herself. Sometimes, it is easier to play the victim and blame others for our unhappiness, but hanging around for others to magically change their attitude towards us is fruitless and only exacerbates our innate sense of helplessness and low self-confidence.

The great implosion

Often people with anxiety will try to avoid heightened emotion at all costs. In Julie's case, she has learned from childhood that expressing emotions only results in rejection. Therefore, she tries to hold them in all the time. However, instead of being 'full up' with this storage of emotion, we tend to feel empty inside or as Julie described: 'a void' and 'a lack of attachment'; she didn't feel anything but numbness and emptiness.

However, we can only suppress our emotions for so long before they rise to the surface. Julie's panic attacks were a manifestation of these strong emotions; the more she tried to contain them, the more attacks she experienced.

The biggest fear for Julie was to lose control; if she started experiencing emotions she was afraid it would become too much, and she feared she would feel overwhelmed and out of control. For passive people like Julie, there is often a huge dread of being caught out and looking stupid; therefore confrontation is avoided at all costs.

The silent assassin

The irony of passive behaviour is that it invites exactly the sort of reaction that the passive person fears the most: criticism and rejection. For example, I felt myself getting frustrated when I was trying to help Julie, but I knew that if she was aware of me losing control of the session, she would retreat even further into herself. Let's face it: if her psychologist couldn't keep himself together, why would she feel encouraged to talk to anyone else about how she was feeling? The last thing I wanted to do was to reinforce the idea that expressing emotion was threatening. That's why I had to lighten the tone of the sessions to ensure she didn't feel under threat.

Although the passive person might not be aware of it, remaining silent is also a form of manipulation as it does nothing else but provoke a reaction from others, usually a negative one. It may be a way of punishing others for rejecting or criticising them. Watching somebody else become frustrated and tongue-tied is somewhat satisfying to a passive person as there is a certain comfort in witnessing someone else feeling as awkward as them.

The angry assassin

As we have seen, those with passive behaviour do not provide themselves with the opportunity to practice the skills to communicate effectively. Similarly, people that communicate in an aggressive way also have poor relationships with others.

Donald's story

During our first session, Donald, an office manager in his early fifties, handed me a letter. 'I'll be putting this in my obituary,' he joked.

It was a letter of complaint from one of his staff members issued to him by the Human Resources (HR) department:

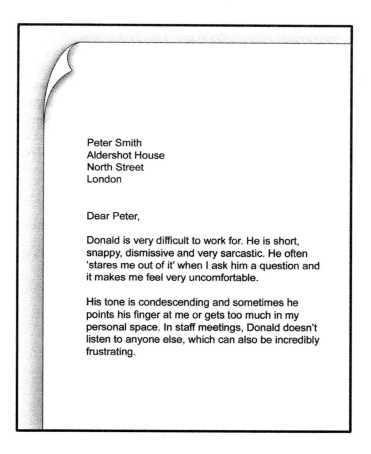

Peter Smith
Aldershot House
North Street
London

Dear Peter,

Donald is very difficult to work for. He is short, snappy, dismissive and very sarcastic. He often 'stares me out of it' when I ask him a question and it makes me feel very uncomfortable.

His tone is condescending and sometimes he points his finger at me or gets too much in my personal space. In staff meetings, Donald doesn't listen to anyone else, which can also be incredibly frustrating.

After I read the letter, I asked Donald to tell me a bit more about the situation at work. He told me that he had been the 'head honcho' in his office for years, but suddenly the company had been taken over by a larger company, and he found himself reporting to more senior people, which he wasn't used to: 'There are too many chiefs in work now and they are treating me like an underling, even though I know more than all of them put together.' Donald was worried about being pushed out as the company expanded. 'I used to call the shots and now nobody listens to me; they just do whatever they want.'

I asked Donald if he was aware of how his behaviour was affecting others. 'Well, I knew I was being a bit abrupt, maybe, but I am a bit of a joker, and I thought that people would also understand that I don't mean anything by it.'

During some role plays, I managed to ascertain Donald's style of communication with his staff and his superiors. In one scenario, Donald was asked to complete an evaluation of several of his staff members in a week. He admitted to reacting with several of the following responses:

> 'Oh right, I'm really going to get that done in a week, aren't I?'
> 'Yeah, that's really going to happen.'
> 'You've got to be kidding. But, hey, if that's what you think, then fine.'

Understandably, his colleagues came away from the conversation feeling dismissed and annoyed. It was numerous comments like this, together with aggressive body language, that had led to an official complaint against him.

Donald felt frustrated in his job and felt he was no longer being listened to. His sarcasm was his way of defending his sense of self-worth at work, albeit unproductively. Rather than being openly aggressive, he was able to cover up his anger by making a joke even though he was seething inside. The problem was that others were picking up on his fury and resented him for it.

The thing is that Donald was trying to minimize the risk of retaliation by being sarcastic, thus making light of the aggression. This meant that if somebody openly confronted him about it, he could defend himself by saying, 'I was only having a laugh.' However, this tactic only lasted for so long. But he did admit to feeling badly about his behaviour:

> 'It is true that in meetings, I go in there, stand at the head of the table and dish out orders. I don't do question or suggestion time. I don't delegate. I suppose this must bother people and I guess I feel bad about that.'

I asked him why he wouldn't let others speak up. After a while, he said it was because he was afraid that if someone else came up with an idea or suggestion, he might not be able to understand what they are talking about; then people would think he was stupid. As long as his sole opinion was never contradicted, he was still able to retain a bit of control and power.

Opening the kimono

Whether the behaviour is passive or aggressive, there is still that tendency to beat ourselves up. The more this happens, the less confident we will feel and will end up acting similarly in every situation. To deal with feelings of inadequacy and rejection, the passive or aggressive person will at times, subconsciously, attempt to make others feel even more inadequate. It doesn't feel as bad if they are not the only under-confident people in the room.

Take Rebecca, for instance, who worked as a financial analyst. She felt that she was being treated unfairly by her managers. They continued to accuse her of not doing her job properly, sent her on courses to brush up her skills, and continued to single her out from the rest of the team. Rebecca was feeling extremely misunderstood and rejected by her managers. She was often tearful and could not understand why she was being treated that way.

The rest of the team tended to 'suck up' to the managers and 'play the hierarchical game'. Rebecca was adamant that she was not going to give her managers the satisfaction of behaving the same way, considering the way that they treated her! She wanted them to know that they were not as great as they thought they were, and wanted them to know how they made her feel about herself. So, she played a silent game, where she sulked whenever they asked her to do something, and kept quiet in meetings even when she had something to contribute. Of course, her managers didn't pick up on her rage at all and just presumed she had some sort of attitude problem. This caused them to continue to treat her 'unfairly'.

Rebecca came to realize that if she wanted to keep the job she enjoyed and fund the lifestyle to which she had become accustomed then she would need to act differently towards her managers. She knew that she would have to change her style of passive-aggressive communication towards them rather than waiting for them to change the way they acted towards her. However, it took her some time to figure out how she could get them to see her in a new light. (Please see Chapter Ten for more information on Procrastination.)

Eventually, she faced her fears of feeling more 'disrespected and rejected' by them by 'playing the game' in a way that benefited her as well as her superiors. She started to ask for their help more often and actively sought their approval on projects she undertook. At first, her efforts to prove herself were rejected, for example, she asked her manager if she could take on a project to prove her ability. Her manager waved her away, and gave it to someone else, but Rebecca found a way of completing a significant part of the project, in her own time, which impressed her boss. In no time at all, her managers started to relate to her in a different way; they stopped 'harassing' her and she felt they were beginning to treat her more fairly.

On the same page

Assertive communication is the most effective way of expressing how we feel in a way that also respects the rights of others. Assertive people are confident people whereas passive and aggressive behaviour is a sign of a lack of confidence.

Being unassertive leads to:

- Loss of self-esteem and self-confidence
- Weaker sense of identity
- Lack of sense of purpose
- Poor communication leading to unhealthy relationships with others
- Psychological distress

So, if we are more assertive, we improve our levels of self-esteem, confidence and communication skills. We are able to feel that we are more in control of our lives. It also helps us to develop more self-awareness, and to realize that we can't blame others for the way we feel and behave. Being assertive is all about taking charge and getting what we want without having to change our entire personalities or sacrifice our beliefs. It stands to reason that if we communicate our intentions more clearly then we have a better chance of achieving our wants and needs.

However, many of us are reluctant to assert ourselves in difficult situations.

Consider how you would feel if a work colleague said the following to you:

> 'I can't believe you messed up that business proposal. You are completely incompetent!'

If you are a passive person, you will internalize the hurt, accept the opinion as fact, say nothing, and walk away. An aggressive person will immediately retaliate in anger, and add fuel to the fire. The chances are either response will leave the person feeling badly about the way they responded; the passive person will wish they had spoken up and defended themselves, and the aggressive person will regret losing the rag with their work colleague.

Of course, it is understandable that if we are told we are stupid or incompetent then it will hurt us inside. However, being assertive is about managing our emotional experience. In the situation above, the assertive person is most likely to respond in the following way:

> 'Thank you for letting me know that you think I'm incompetent; I will think about that. I do feel quite upset that you said that, though, because I tend to think that you are attacking me. However, I will take it on board.'

This might seem to be an odd way to respond to an insult but it is the most assertive way to do it. You come away from the situation with your dignity in tact and because you reacted so gracefully, your work colleague is more likely to have a re-think about making the same comment a second time.

Assertiveness boot camp

One of the best steps towards becoming more assertive is to practise. It is a skill like any other and requires a certain amount of training. In Julie's case, I started her off with a number of challenges to encourage her to confront some of her fears. For example, Julie had bought a skirt but when she tried it on at home, she realized it was a bit too big for her. She was afraid to return it in case the people in the shop would think she was stupid for buying it in the first place.

So, I set her a task: to return the item by a date we both agreed on. She completed the task and was pleased with her achievement. The shop staff had turned out to be pleasant, helpful, and friendly, and, of course, didn't think anything of her returning the skirt.

You might think that achieving a goal like this is insignificant; however, taking steps to confront situations that make us feel uncomfortable is an important way of building up our confidence and making us more assertive. Assertive people tend to be much less anxious in awkward situations.

Below are some other scenarios that Julie perceived as being uncomfortable. Have a read through and see if you can relate to any of them:

- Questioning a bill
- Returning food in a restaurant
- Accepting/turning down a date
- Confronting someone who skips her in the queue
- Initiating conversations with others
- Asking for the return of a borrowed item
- Requesting a favour
- Inability to say 'no' without apologising profusely
- Telling her boss she cannot make a deadline/has too much work on

Many of us may be able to identify with some of the above situations and also perceive them as uncomfortable; however, no matter how awkward the situation might be; if we are assertive enough, we will be able to tackle each one in the right way.

If confronting some of the situations above seems a little intimidating at first, then try a few simple exercises to challenge yourself. Perhaps you could say 'Good Morning' to a stranger or knock on your neighbour's door on the pretext of borrowing an item. Positively engaging with others, even on the smallest level, is a real step towards building up your confidence.

Managing the message

When we are assertive, we are communicating the message about what we think and feel about a certain situation. It is about communicating a statement about our personal experience in a non-aggressive, non-passive way. Of course, a little aggression can be useful when handling some difficult situations but only if it is used appropriately.

If somebody disagrees with you, then you must handle it in such a way that the other person knows that you are ready to listen to their view and work towards a compromise, if necessary.

Again, the language we use is vital when we are trying to get our message across. Assertive people use statements that are clear and to the point such as:

> 'I like'
> 'I feel'
> 'I don't like'
> 'I would like'
> 'I think'

These 'I' statements help to reaffirm your needs whilst 'You' statements tend to shift the focus on to the other person thus distracting from your needs. Additionally, this sort of language helps to avoid blaming, criticising, or accusing the other person.

Communication killers

If we are upset by others, it is tempting to fall into more accusatory language and statements. However, this only leads to communication breakdown and further damage to the relationship. So, next time you find yourself becoming a bit wound up, make an effort to stay away from the following statements:

> 'You're really annoying me'
> 'You always behave like this'
> 'You should have done this better'
> 'You'd better sort yourself out'
> 'I'm not the problem, you are'
> 'Why the hell did you do that?'
> 'Typical sensitive woman'
> 'You're not leaving until you sort your mess out'

The right sort of assertive language is also useful to separate the experience from the person. For example, 'I feel upset when I notice you interrupt me', is a far more constructive way of expressing how you feel. Conversely, by saying: 'You always interrupt me; what's wrong with you?' you are launching an attack on the person's character and, therefore, they are more likely to take the comment personally i.e., that they are the sort of person who always interrupts people. Of course, the person is more likely to go on the defensive in this instance and begin a counter attack, leading to a heated argument, and potentially, communication breakdown.

No means no

Some of us find it difficult to say no, especially in our demanding working environments, where saying no to a senior person can be one way to knock you off the career ladder. However, sometimes it's more the idea of saying the 'n' word that causes our anxiety. Most people exaggerate the consequences of saying no, and therefore don't even attempt it. Assertive people are those who are aware of their own limitations and have the ability to communicate them in a certain way. They are often respected by others and considered comfortable to be around, even when they do not necessarily meet the needs of others. When I asked Julie what would happen if she said 'no' to her boss, she told me:

> 'He will think I am being rude and will give me an even harder time. I know he doesn't really like me, but he will like me even less if I say no to him'.

Like Julie, many of us believe that when we say no, we are rejecting the person rather than the request. However, the chances are Julie's boss is not going to take her refusal personally, but simply take what she is saying at face value. As Julie has an excellent track record and a reputation for working hard, he will most likely think to himself: OK, Julie can't take the work on; I'll have to give it to someone else.

There are many different ways of saying 'no'. Sometimes we can take a rain check: 'I can't attend the meeting this afternoon but let's reschedule for next week.' Or simply: 'No thanks, I don't have time for lunch today.' Whatever method you choose, just ensure you don't pepper your response with the word 'sorry'. Too many apologies put you at a disadvantage and weaken your stance.

The best way to saying no is to anticipate the situation. For example, we all know that weekly work meetings are mainly about delegating tasks among the team. If you are genuinely drowning in work, then be upfront about it the minute the topic arises and make sure you have all your facts in place: 'I'm completely swamped at the moment; I have four deadlines over the next two weeks so I am unable to fit anything else into my schedule'. This is a concise, clear statement, backed up by evidence and there is very little others can say to persuade you to take on more work.

In the office, both Donald and Julie struggled with saying no to a constant flow of work with impossible deadlines. Despite each of them explaining to their respective bosses that they were swamped, it seemed like they were being ignored. Julie would accept the work and say nothing, whereas Donald would also take on the work but make a sarcastic and angry comment about it. They would then beat themselves up about the way they had responded.

Here is the assertive response both Julie and Donald practised:

> Boss: 'I want this proposal in a week's time.'
> Julie/Donald: 'I feel anxious when you ask me if I can get things done in a week. I think that you haven't heard me when I tell you how much work I have on. I'm not sure if I can get it done in a week but I will certainly try.'

This is an honest response about how you are feeling about the situation; it also lets your boss know that you will do your best and are open to negotiation.

The first time Julie made this statement to her boss, he was so shocked that she had spoken up for herself that it took him a while to respond. Eventually, he granted her a two-day extension and treated her with a little more consideration the next time he needed a quick turnaround on a project.

Donald, too, found this way better than his usual sarcastic remarks. He found it a relief that there was a way to let his work colleagues and superiors know how he felt about the situation without feeling obliged to mask his irritation behind the sarcasm.

Down to you

Becoming more assertive requires a great deal of self-awareness. We need to be aware of how our own thoughts lead to our feelings and behaviour. Have a look at the following tips and think about what you might need to do in order to adjust your behaviour:

It's all in the tone

Tone of voice very much comes into play when we are trying to get our message across. Be aware that others will be immediately able to pick up on an edge in your voice and will not be as conducive to giving you a positive response.

Speak up!

'Speaking up' is not just an expression for putting forward your point of view; take it at its literal meaning and make sure your voice is loud enough to be heard and that it is firm but relaxed.

Body talk

Make sure your body language is also receptive. Getting in some-one else's personal space or finger pointing is a definite no-no. Keep your head up and maintain eye contact (without staring). Try and keep on the same eye level as the other person, for example, if your boss approaches you while you are sitting at your desk, stand up so you are both on an even keel. Standing tall at an appropriate distance, with your arms relaxed (rather than crossed) means you are open for a fair discussion.

Pay attention

Listening can be an art in itself. However, making it clear that you actually want to hear what the other person thinks is often the difference between a blazing row and a happy ending. Butting in when someone else is trying to make a point only exacerbates the situation. Similarly, trying to offer solutions halfway through a heated discussion can make the other person feel like they are not being heard.

Donald openly admitted he wasn't the best listener when it came to his staff; however, he tried to hold meetings where he wasn't the only voice in the room and found that his colleagues had some excellent suggestions which he found easy to understand, and was able to put into practise straight away.

Assertiveness skills: Dos and Don'ts

So, if there is a situation at work or at home that you would like to confront, consider the following dos and don'ts:

- *Do* prepare what you are going to say; write it down beforehand and rehearse it several times. This will prevent you from becoming tongue-tied when the moment arrives.
- *Don't* think that assertiveness is all about winning. Remember that it is about compromise, letting the other person know that your needs conflict with theirs but you are still open to negotiation.
- *Do* practise 'I feel' and 'I think' statements with the appropriate emotion and thought: 'I feel upset because I think …;' is a great way of expressing how your thoughts lead to emotions within yourself and towards others.
- *Don't* be discouraged if the other person starts to criticize you: 'Well, I would cut you a bit more slack if you weren't so late all the time.' Accepting criticism (if it is true) and letting the other person know that you are open to change is the best way of retaining your self-confidence: 'Yes, it is true that I am late sometimes, but I will try my best to be on time from now on.'
- *Do* question critical comments that you believe might be unfair: 'You probably won't get on with that client as they are a bit sensitive and you're not the most tactful person in the world, are you?' You could respond: 'In what way do you think I'm tactless?' If the other person can provide you with some examples then at least you know the criticism is constructive and there is something you can change about your behaviour.
- *Don't* encourage the speaker when you want to say no. Nodding, asking questions, or agreeing with them indicates that you are interested in taking on the task and you will end up finding it more difficult to refuse them. Keep your tone firm but relaxed and your body language still.

Buying in

We have all come across people at work that behave in a passive or aggressive manner. This can be difficult in a working environment as it causes tension and divisions in the team. Working in an office is all about communication, whether it is in general meetings or one-to-ones etc., so it is vital that everybody gets along.

So, if you have somebody on your team that seems extremely quiet, keeps the head down and doesn't say a word, rather than ignoring them, try and encourage them to come out of their shell.

There is a way of being curious without being invasive. Ask if they had a good weekend or if they had seen a particular programme on television that was on the previous night etc. Start off with small, general enquiries and if they seem a bit quiet at first, then persevere. Over time, the chances are they might open up a bit.

Similarly, you may find that approaching an aggressive person is almost as off putting as dealing with a passive one; however, it is important that you are very clear (by using assertive and non-accusatory statements) about the effect of their behaviour on the team.

The upshot

The more assertive we are the more confident we will feel. Effective and assertive communication is the only way to get what we want whilst respecting the rights of others. More importantly, it provides us with the self-awareness and self-esteem we need to be able to cope with the countless stressful and difficult work situations we encounter each day.

Julie learned not to internalize everything and came to the conclusion that if she lost her job, it wouldn't be the end of the world. By adopting new ways to communicate, Donald also began to see an improvement in his relationships at home and at work.

Although both Donald and Julie struggled with the way they related to others, by taking steps to address their own behaviours, they began to receive more favourable responses.

Being assertive is all about noticing what *you* can do differently to change the situation that you are in; it takes practise. Persevere and watch your confidence grow; you will soon see some great results.

CHAPTER NINE

The rise and fall

"If you can't sleep, then get up and do something instead of lying there worrying. It's the worry that gets you, not the lack of sleep."

—Dale Carnegie

S leep is something we absolutely cannot do without, yet most of us take it for granted. Given that we can go longer without food than sleep, perhaps it is time to take our sleeping habits a bit more seriously. Our body relies on sleep for growth and repair, and our brain depends on sleep for memory and concentration. Sleeping difficulties have also been found as a symptom of depression and anxiety, and vice versa. Therefore, a good night's sleep is essential if we want to maintain our mental and physical health.

The sleep illusion

Many of us worry about sleep, fearing that if we don't get enough then it will have catastrophic effects on our ability to function normally. However, there are general beliefs out there that aren't necessarily accurate:

'I have to get at least 8 hours a night'

There is no such thing as the 'right' amount of sleep; it is very much an individual thing and differs from person to person. The body will take all the sleep it needs. Some people need between seven and nine hours per night, and others may feel refreshed after only four or five hours. It is not about the amount we sleep but the quality of it. Remember that our sleeping patterns also change as we get older. You may have been a 'sleeping machine' when you were in your twenties but you will find yourself sleeping less when you are in your sixties.

'The more sleep the better'

It is not necessarily healthy to get more than the average eight hours per night; oversleeping can leave you feeling sluggish and, ironically, tired, the next day. Research has also shown that oversleeping is linked to weight gain and obesity.

'A few nights without sleep is dangerous'

Many people believe that going without sleep is going to make them ill or affect their performance the following day. However, it is absolutely possible to function perfectly well, even after a night of tossing and turning, as long as that behaviour doesn't persist. Thus, there is no harm in losing a few nights sleep, but if it becomes an ongoing problem then it is wise to address the underlying reasons behind the lack of sleep.

'I'll never sleep well again!'

Everybody experiences sleep difficulties at one stage or another; life-changing events such as bereavement or even moving house can upset our sleep patterns. However, in most cases, sleep disturbance is really only temporary and it does pass relatively quickly. Of course, if we worry all the time about our inability to fall asleep, we will end up delaying the return to a normal sleeping pattern.

'I didn't sleep a wink last night!'

When we have a bad night, we sometimes believe we didn't get any sleep at all. However, research has shown that even people with insomnia actually sleep longer than they think. So, even if you have sleeping difficulties, the chances are you will drop off for a longer period than you realize.

Max's story

Max is a head trader for a top American investment bank in the City. Every morning, he gets up at 4 am and drives an hour to get to his office. He is at his desk at 6 am in preparation for the opening of the international stock exchanges. When the markets open, Max stays glued to his screen for twelve hours, trading and making calls. His work requires intense concentration and a will of iron. If he is not on the ball, Max has the potential to lose the bank millions of dollars.

Because of the intensity of his job, Max knows he cannot afford to lose a night's sleep. Every minute of the day is precious. He goes to bed at 8 pm and takes a sleeping tablet to help him settle down. After some months, Max gets into a routine of taking a pill to help him sleep. One night, Max can't get to sleep; he lies awake tossing and turning so he takes another pill, but that doesn't work either. The following day he goes into work, feeling sleepy and dazed. He buys a stock instead of selling it and makes an immediate loss on the market. In a panic, he manages to bring the trade back from the point of no return and recovers the loss. Nobody knows what has happened but Max panics anyway. When he gets home that evening, he is so worried about making a similar mistake the next day that he takes three sleeping pills; he does sleep, but fitfully, and still feels 'out of it' when he wakes up.

As the weeks go by, Max begins to dread the evenings. Furthermore, new neighbours have moved in across the hall from his apartment and they are fond of throwing mid-week parties. Max makes up his mind that he will have to go to bed before the noise starts so he can sleep through without being disturbed, but this doesn't work either. Max becomes afraid of going to bed in case he is unable to sleep; his bedroom has become a prison. At the weekends, he cancels all his social engagements as he is too tired and down to go out with his friends.

As Max becomes more sleep deprived, he begins to lose concentration and his ability to remember essential market information. The final straw is when Max is sent on the red eye to New York on business for two days. When he comes home, he suffers from intense jetlag and ends up catching the flu. All of this on top of his sleeping difficulties is too much for him to bear, and he takes two weeks off sick to recover. These are his first sick days in five years.

When Max returns to work, he still feels a bit shaky and is still suffering from sleeping difficulties. That's when he decides to get some help.

Thinking twice

During our session, I asked Max about the type of thoughts running through his head when he was trying to get to sleep. This is what he told me (I have underlined the anxious language that he uses):

> 'When I check the clock and see how late it is, I feel really anxious. My mind is racing and I feel really agitated. I think to myself, I *should* be asleep by now; if I don't sleep tonight, I will be a wreck in the morning. If I'm a wreck then I won't perform at my optimum level. *What if* I make terrible mistakes? I will lose my company a huge amount of money. Then I will lose my job, and no-one else will hire me, and my life will be over ...'

Of course, this all might sound a bit dramatic, but think about it, when we are awake in the dead of night, all alone, don't we all find ourselves having catastrophic thoughts? Being awake at all hours is very isolating. When we feel there is nobody around that can give us comfort or provide a distraction, our thoughts tend to spiral out of control. When this happens, we become anxious, and as soon as our body detects the anxiety, it sends a rush of adrenalin which only ends up keeping us awake.

In short, worrying about not sleeping is a worry in itself. So, how do we tackle these anxious thoughts? Well, for starters, it's useful to create your own inner dialogue to challenge those catastrophic thoughts:

> 'I'm not sleeping but that's ok for now. I will hopefully sleep a little better tomorrow.'

This means that we are more accepting of the fact we are not sleeping, which makes us feel less distressed.

'If I don't sleep well, I may be a little tired, but I will be able to function the next day. It might not be the best I have ever performed, but I will be able to manage.'

Again, this is another way of accepting our predicament. We are telling ourselves that it may not be ideal to be tired, but it's ok.

However, it is important that we don't blame our sleeping difficulties for our problems. For example, Max believed that his worry and anxiety would disappear as soon as he had a good night's sleep, or as he put it: 'It's because I can't sleep that everything is really bad at the moment. My noisy neighbours are also a contributing factor.' Of course, it wasn't his noisy neighbours or his sleep pattern that were the cause of his problem, but his thoughts about them and his underlying anxiety needed to be addressed.

No-brainer

So, as we have mentioned, there are usually underlying reasons why we can't sleep. Like Max, we may be worried or anxious about events the next day, or we may use our bedtime as a means of ruminating over what has already occurred.

Either way, it is far better to address the underlying distress behind our sleeping difficulties than to rely on sleeping pills. Taking a sleeping aid is a way of externalising the problem. The more pills we take, the less we learn how to manage the distress by ourselves. Therefore, we end up avoiding coping on our own. Of course, this has an effect on our self-confidence as we end up feeling 'weak' that we needed to turn to pills in the first place.

In Max's case, the more anxious he became, the more pills he took until he became addicted. He felt that the only way he could cope was to take them every night. However, Max suffered from anxiety which had an effect on his sleep, but by taking the pills he was depending on them, rather than himself, to take away his anxiety.

The problem with sleeping pills is that they are really only a short term measure. If we are anxious enough, we are able to overpower the strength of any sleeping pill. This is why we think they are not 'working' anymore. In fact, many of the side-effects of taking sleeping pills mimic the same symptoms of a poor night's sleep. For example, Max complained about feeling drowsy, dizzy and fuzzy-headed and put it down to a lack of sleep the previous night. However, it is more likely that he experienced these symptoms as a result of the pills he took to help him sleep.

Kicking the tyres

So, if you are planning on coming off sleeping pills, keep the following in mind:

- Make sure you come off them gradually over a period of time. This is something you can work out with your doctor.
- Withdrawal from medication can sometimes have a number of side-effects in the short term. Don't panic! These are only temporary symptoms and will fade in time.
- Take your mind off the side-effects by keeping yourself busy. Focusing on how you're feeling all the time will only exacerbate the problem.
- Note down any side-effects of the pills, withdrawal symptoms, and details of your sleeping pattern. This will help your doctor work out the best schedule for you to come off the pills.
- If your doctor agrees, then try substituting your sleeping pills for herbal pills. This may help with the weaning process.

The 50,000 foot view

Like many City executives who often travel, Max suffers from severe jetlag. There is no magic cure for jetlag but there are ways you can manage it to limit its effects. As we know, when we cross different time zones, our bodies find it difficult to adjust to the different rhythms of day and night. Some people take a couple of days to get over jetlag, but others can take up to two weeks to feel fully functional again.

Symptoms of jetlag include:

- Fatigue
- Loss of appetite
- Headache
- Irregular sleep patterns
- Insomnia
- Disorientation
- Grogginess
- Confusion
- Reduced memory/concentration
- Irritability
- Mild depression

So, with all that to deal with, it makes sense to make an effort to minimize the effects of jetlag before you go on a long journey. So, here are some tips for overcoming jetlag:

- Set your watch to the time at your destination as soon as you get on the plane. This is a psychological method that will help to prepare your mind for the time difference.
- Get up and wander around the cabin and do some exercises as often as you can. This will stop your body from becoming stiff and tired.
- Don't eat too much or drink alcohol and coffee on the flight as this will delay the adjustment process. Drink plenty of water and eat in moderation.
- If your flight is through the night, then try and sleep as much as you can. This will give you a good head start when you reach your destination.
- Pack some earplugs! Blocking out the noise will help you relax much more quickly. Also use an eye mask to shade your eyes from the light.
- Once you arrive, make sure you comply with the local time. It is more difficult to stay up if you get there in the morning, but it is essential to try to keep awake until nightfall.
- If you are hungry, then eat meals that are most suited to that time of day; for example, if you get in at 8am, order some breakfast (even if it is dinner time at home!).
- Go to bed early and keep a snack close by, just in case your body starts screaming for food at 3am.

- As soon as you get to your hotel, have a hot shower. Not only will it brighten you up after your flight, and help to keep you awake, but it will raise your body temperature which may have decreased after a long journey.

Rise and shine!

Some people have difficulty falling asleep and others fall asleep quickly but might wake up a couple of hours later and find it hard to go back to sleep again. Irrespective of the category you fall into, if you can't sleep, then get up! It is important to disassociate your bed with unrest and distress!

We have a tendency to think that if we get up, then we will waste the time we would spend on trying to sleep, but this is untrue. If you have to get up in the middle of the night, then don't think it's the end of the world. It is better to get up after 15 or 20 minutes than to lie there for hours, fretting, and ruminating about the situation.

When you are up and about, do something un-stimulating that will distract you from thinking about the fact you are not sleeping. Don't start working or doing anything too stimulating even if you are feeling really bright and alert. This will train your body and mind into believing that you are ready to work at that time of the day, and you will end up waking up at that time every morning.

So, make sure you avoid anything that is stimulating when your aim is to return to bed: pick up a book (preferably a boring one) and read for a while, watch an un-stimulating DVD or do a bit of ironing; anything 'boring' or mentally and physically inactive enough to make those eyelids droop. Don't be tempted to do any exercise if you want to get back to sleep. Only go back to bed if you feel sleepy; if you still can't sleep, then just get up again and do some more reading or any other mundane or inactive task. Continue this process until you find yourself ready to sleep.

Similarly, if you wake up earlier than your alarm clock, then call it a night, and get up. For example, sometimes Max would wake up at 3 am and just stay in bed, tossing and turning, worried about losing a precious hour's sleep. However, if you wake up an hour or two early, then try to accept the fact that you are going to have an early start. Don't get up and go back to bed. Although it's the last thing you might feel like, try and do some exercise if you have time to kill. This will give you enough energy to get through the day and will help to tire you out for the following night.

Peace of mind

There are several ways we can put our worries to bed before we settle down for the evening. The following are simple exercises that will help to calm a racing mind and prepare us for a good night's sleep.

Sleep diary

Keeping a sleep diary is an excellent way of establishing the reasons why you having trouble sleeping. Although a racing mind comes into play, others areas like our diet, our caffeine intake, our alcohol intake, and types of medication can also affect the way we sleep; thus it is also useful to note down some facts and information about the sort of day you have had before bedtime.

So, grab a pen and paper, and set a couple of minutes aside each morning to fill in some answers to the following questions, regarding your sleep pattern, from the night before:

- What time did you go to bed last night?
- What time did you wake up this morning?
- How long did it take you to fall asleep?
- How often did you wake up during the night?
- Did you take any sleeping pills/medication?
- How did you feel when you woke up? (Refreshed, tired, exhausted)

Now, take a look at the below and complete the answers to the questions *every evening* before you go to bed:

- Did you have any exercise today? If so, how long did you exercise for?

- How much caffeine did you have during the day? (For example: coffee, tea, chocolate, soft drinks etc.)
- How much alcohol did you consume during the day?
- Did you have a nap? If so, how long was it for?
- How tired did you feel today?

Depending on your answers, there could be a direct link between your behaviour during the day and your sleeping habits. When Max went through these questions, he was, immediately, able to address some of the areas that were contributing to his anxiety and sleeping difficulties. For example, because Max was taking sleeping pills, he would often wake up the next morning feeling tired and sluggish. He would then drink endless cups of coffee to wake himself up again. However, the amount of caffeine he was taking into his system was pumping him with adrenalin, making it more difficult for him to settle down at bedtime. Therefore, Max decided to cut down his coffee consumption to a couple of cups a day, which he would have during the early morning only. Max also cut down on the amount of alcohol he drank during the week, and regulated himself to drinking in moderation at the weekend only.

He also realized that he wasn't doing enough exercise during the day. Being a trader meant that he was tied to his desk so he ended up sitting down for hours on end. However, Max decided that he would make time for a jog in the early morning before work and soon found that he had more energy during the day as a result.

What keeps you awake at night ...

As we have seen, sleep difficulties are linked to anxiety and depression. If we worry excessively before bedtime, the chances are we are going to still be anxious about the problem when we are lying in bed. So, the key is to put our worries to one side before bedtime.

So, if you have something on your mind, then write down your worries and thoughts and ways you feel you can address the problem. This is similar to the problem solving technique used in Chapter Seven.

The following is an extract from Max's notebook:

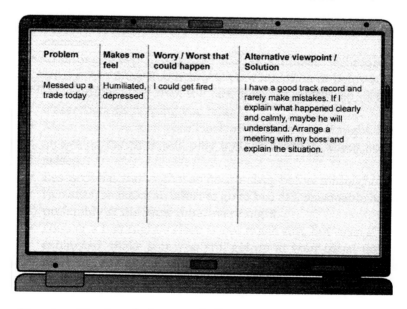

Problem	Makes me feel	Worry / Worst that could happen	Alternative viewpoint / Solution
Noisy neighbours	Frustrated, angry	Get a bad night's sleep and make mistakes at work	Even if there is still noise and I don't sleep well, it doesn't mean I will make terrible mistakes at work. Talk to my neighbours and ask them to keep the noise down. Wear earplugs.

Problem	Makes me feel	Worry / Worst that could happen	Alternative viewpoint / Solution
Messed up a trade today	Humiliated, depressed	I could get fired	I have a good track record and rarely make mistakes. If I explain what happened clearly and calmly, maybe he will understand. Arrange a meeting with my boss and explain the situation.

Exercises like these help us to challenge our thoughts and worries and to find ways of taking steps to resolve the problem, rather than ruminating over it. Eventually, Max did have a chat with his neighbours and although they were amazed that he went to bed so early, they agreed to make an effort to keep the noise down. As a result of taking some action to address the problem, Max felt a bit more in control and less frustrated about the situation.

Similarly, Max's boss was more understanding than Max had predicted, and he came away from the meeting relieved and more confident in his own abilities to perform well.

Thus, simple exercises like this can really make a difference to the way we think, and also help to tame a racing mind. For example, Max had a habit about worrying that he would forget to carry out a task the following day, so I suggested that he jot down a 'To do' list a couple of hours before bedtime, outlining his plans for the following day. I also mentioned that he would be better off separating himself from the list by leaving it in another room so he wouldn't be tempted to check it all the time.

Writing down a 'To do' list helps to put our mind at rest and lessens that fear we have that we will forget to do something. If we still find ourselves worrying, then keep a pen and paper by your bed and jot them down during the night.

Fail to plan and plan to fail

One of the reasons that Max couldn't sleep was because he tended to squeeze so much into a day that he was too wound up to rest when he got home. He was so committed to his job that he rarely saw his friends and was unable to sustain a relationship.

However, when we really broke down Max's working day, it was clear that he wasn't managing his time effectively. You might think there is no such thing as effective time management in such an intense environment as the trading floor; however, there are ways in which you can manage your time successfully without sacrificing the quality of your work.

The main point of time management is to allow ourselves the time to do the things that we enjoy and value in life. So here's how you do it:

- Write down your goals and priorities in life. You may think you haven't time to do this but this is a significant step towards successful time management. Then prioritize those goals, think about which ones are the most important, and rank them accordingly.

- Take one of the goals and plan it out, step by step. For example, Max really missed having a girlfriend and was keen to be in a relationship. As he didn't feel he had enough time to go out socially in the evenings, he decided to join a dating website. This meant that he could arrange dates when it suited him and gave him an evening out to look forward to.
- Delegate tasks at work: don't do everything yourself. Max realized that he wasn't making the best use out of his assistant, preferring to do everything himself. However, he began to distribute work, which freed up some time for him during the working day. (Please see Chapter Four for more information on delegation.).
- Be as organized as you can. Max tended to work in an 'organized mess' at work and at home. However, being surrounded by disorder only adds to the frustration and tension, and wastes time.
- Identify those areas where you can save time. In Max's case, he realized he was spending too much time taking personal calls during office hours. Thus, he told those callers to contact him after work only, or if it was urgent, then to text or email instead.
- Think about the time of day where you excel the most. Mornings are usually the best time to do work, whereas our performance usually fades a bit in the afternoons. Either way, we are not always 'switched on' to the highest setting, so we need to dedicate the most challenging tasks when we feel the most active; and the easier tasks for when we feel less energised.
- Don't put off unpleasant tasks until the next day, tempting though it may be. Instead, allocate a certain amount of time for the task and promise yourself a reward when you successfully complete it. (Please see Chapter Ten for some more information on Procrastination)
- Revisit your work diary and ensure there is enough space in it to give you time to do your job effectively. For example, Max had so many back-to-back meetings after the markets closed, that he felt like he was chasing his tail the whole time. Freeing up his diary gave him the leeway to complete the tasks he needed to do.
- Achieve a work-life balance by setting a suitable amount of time for enjoyable activities outside work. Also try and take breaks during the working day: go for a walk, or to the gym. Make the most of your weekends, and when you're on holidays, although this may seem difficult: leave that Blackberry at home!

Tips for sleeping like a log

The key to a good night's sleep is to get your body and mind into a relaxed state. In other words, too much stimulation before you go to bed will have a negative effect on your sleep. So, how do you prepare yourself for bedtime?

- Exercise early in the day rather than in the evening.
- If you are working from home, switch off your laptop/Blackberry at least two hours before bedtime.
- Avoid heavy meals or spicy food at night. This will just sit in your stomach and affect your ability to sleep. Some people even find that a banana before bedtime helps them sleep!
- Choose herbal teas or a milky drink instead of caffeinated, to help you settle down.
- Listen to relaxing music, or take a hot bath/shower before bed.
- Muscular relaxation, meditation, and breathing exercises are also extremely useful when it comes to settling the mind and the body. (Please see Appendices I, II, and III for some examples of these exercises.)
- Counting sheep may sound like an outdated technique but it works! Anything that distracts your attention or helps you focus on anything other than the fact that you can't sleep, is one step closer towards helping you relax.
- Make sure you turn your clock away from you at night. Keeping an eye on the clock will only fuel your anxiety about not falling asleep.
- Research has shown that an hour's sleep before midnight is worth two after, so make an effort to go to bed at a reasonable hour, and preferably at the same time, every night.
- Having a bad night's sleep is not much fun, but even if you are exhausted, make sure you still get up at your usual time every morning, and avoid napping during the day if possible.
- Look out for natural remedies such as lavender oil; a few drops on your pillow every night will help to settle you down.
- Noise at bedtime can be very frustrating, but if it is something you can't easily fix, like road traffic or passing trains, then there is no point getting angry about it. Wear earplugs or do some

relaxation and breathing exercises to try and take your mind off the disturbance.

- Think about what your bed means to you. It is essential that you associate your bed for sleeping, and possible love-making, only. Cut out any other activity that you may carry out in the bedroom such as watching TV, working or eating in bed etc. These activities will only distract you from the main event: falling asleep.

- Take steps to ensure your bedroom environment is as comfortable as it can be. This means checking the air temperature isn't too warm and that you have proper ventilation. Make sure you also have a decent mattress, and comfortable pillows.

- Keep your bedroom as dark as possible. Research has shown that even the tiniest chink of light from the window or an alarm clock has the potential to disrupt sleep.

- Writing down our thoughts and worries is a good way of setting our minds at rest. Make time early in the evening, just for a short period, to scribble down a brief account of the day and any problems that you feel might need to be addressed.

The upshot

Max gradually came off the sleeping pills and made adjustments to his lifestyle, all of which helped him get a good night's sleep. He also spent time addressing his own anxieties and worries by challenging his thoughts and writing down his problems. He soon found he no longer dreaded bedtime. He realized that it wasn't the end of the world if he didn't get a full night's sleep, or if he made an error at work.

Sleep is fundamental to our wellbeing but there is always an underlying reason that we have sleeping problems; making adjustments to our lifestyle certainly helps the sleeping process but if we don't address the real reasons as to why we can't sleep, these lifestyle changes will only take us so far.

CHAPTER TEN

Stranger in the room

"A wise man should consider that health is the greatest of human blessings, and learn how by his own thought to derive benefit from his illness."

—Socrates

Have you ever had a surprise house guest? You know, the doorbell rings late at night; everybody looks at each other to see if anyone is expecting a caller and, when everyone looks as mystified as you, someone makes a move towards the door. On the doorstep with more baggage than the entire lost luggage section of Heathrow airport is Aunt Mabel. You're so shocked to see her that you lose the power of speech for a few seconds; the last time you saw Aunt Mabel, she was boarding a plane to Australia, about ten years ago.

When you come to your senses, your heart sinks; you don't even like Aunt Mabel; she is an alcoholic and smokes like a trooper, not a great influence for your young children. As you usher her into the living room, there is a palpable silence followed by an audible groan. When you ask Aunt Mabel how long she is staying, she just shrugs

175

her shoulders. The rest of the family exchange dismayed looks; she could be hanging around the house forever!

As predicted, Aunt Mabel is a very annoying house guest; she never clears up after herself; smokes in the bathroom; and drinks gin from midday to midnight. You feel a bit hopeless about the situation, but what can you do? You're stuck with her now.

Eventually, the whole family decides to call a crisis meeting and decides how they can work around Aunt Mabel's annoying habits. A semblance of peace is restored but there is still that threatening undercurrent of her presence.

An unwelcome guest

An unexpected serious health diagnosis is like an unwelcome house guest. First of all, you get a shock when it arrives, and then you are left to figure out how you are going to deal with it. Suddenly, there's something else in your life, like Aunt Mabel, an unwanted, uninvited extra presence that you need to cope with.

I wanted to make this analogy to really emphasize one of the most important factors of having a serious illness: it may be a part of you but it does not define who you are. For example, when Gavin, a highly driven IT project manager, was diagnosed with prostate cancer, he felt he was defined by the disease:

> 'In my mind, I would always think this disease was my problem, and I was the one that would have to deal with it, on my own. At work, people would look through me, as if I was a ghost, or refuse to look me in the eye. Suddenly, I went from 'Gav, the IT whiz' to 'Gavin, the bloke with cancer'.

Over time, Gavin came to realize that the disease, like an unwelcome guest, was nothing to do with him as a person. It was a separate issue that also had an effect on everyone around him, whether it was at work or at home. Just like the family who was struggling to cope with Aunt Mabel's annoying ways, Gavin realized that if he was going to battle his cancer, he would need to get together with his own family and those closest to him at work, to figure out how they were going to tackle the situation as a unit.

Although many of us dislike irritable guests, we don't generally ignore them, no matter how much we would like to; we usually make an effort to listen to what the guest wants and needs, but most of us are loathe to let inconvenient guests overpower our way of life or intrude on our relationships.

Similarly, with illness, we need to make space for it and figure out what others can do to help, without it taking over everybody's lives. Sometimes, it's nice to take a break from the illness; to make a conscious decision that once a week, the whole family is not going to even talk about the cancer, to get away from it all for a little while. Then on another day, you can all talk about what the cancer 'wants' and give it the 'air time' that it demands. The point is that dealing with illness isn't just a one-man job; those closest to you may also be affected and need to join together to deal with it, as a separate entity.

Shooting the messenger

It is always a shock to find out you have an illness. As those in the medical field are trained to give the worst case scenario so you are aware of all the risks, there is a natural tendency to second-guess the worst. But it doesn't mean that all those symptoms are going to affect you, although it can seem like you are getting all the bad news at once.

As Gavin told me: 'When I heard the 'C' word from my GP, it was like being punched in the stomach; I just went completely numb all over. As if that wasn't bad enough, he started telling me all the side-effects of the medication he was going to put me on. When I managed to regain my senses, I got really angry with him.'

Gavin's reaction is completely normal. There is a tendency to shoot the messenger when we receive bad news. When I worked in a HIV clinic I was terrified when I had to tell someone that they were HIV positive. I felt like I was the grim reaper, foretelling their destiny. Of course, patients became angry with me; it's far easier to blame someone else rather than dealing with the horror of the actual diagnosis.

If we become angry when we receive a diagnosis, it is really a sign that we are overwhelmed by the news itself. Rather than accept the diagnosis, we externalize the problem by putting the blame on the messenger. As we know, anger is our instinctive way of dealing with a perceived threat to our self-worth. For some of us, it may seem like a helpful survival mechanism to get angry so that we can fight off the threat. It sometimes seems easier to focus on and be angry with something else than to deal with the actual diagnosis. However, the diagnosed person soon comes to realize that externalising the causality of the threat is pointless and only leads to more psychological distress. The threat is not outside of us but inside, part of our physical self. As we know, the more distressed we become, the more we may, in fact, exacerbate any physical symptoms that we have in relation to our diagnosed condition.

It really took me a good while to come to terms with being the harbinger of doom while working in the HIV clinic, but I finally figured out that I, just like the patients, had to separate myself from the diagnosis. I was simply the person relaying the news; I wasn't the scapegoat; the news itself was a separate entity. It wasn't about me or my life or how people perceived me; it didn't matter if I was upset when giving bad news or happy when giving good news. The delivery of the diagnosis was nothing to do with me as a person; my job was to help others accept it, and suggest ways in which they, with the support of friends and family, could deal with it.

The point is that when you receive a diagnosis, it has nothing to do with the person giving you the news, but all about how you handle your own experience. Let's face it, if we get angry with the GP, what good will it do? We are still left with the diagnosis. It is better to conserve that energy and channel it into something more productive, like figuring out how you're going to deal with the problem.

Between a rock and a hard place

Gavin was a bit of a perfectionist, and had a really difficult time accepting that he had prostate cancer. Typically, perfectionists have a harder time dealing with diagnoses as they regard health problems as a sign of weakness, inadequacy, and failure. Gavin was a workaholic and when he discovered he would have to take time off for treatment, he completely panicked. He was so consumed by his job that he couldn't bear the thought of not being there every day. Without work, he was nothing.

Gavin tried taking a couple of days off work, but hated being at home. He felt useless and unproductive and felt he had to be constantly active to distract himself from his illness. The problem was he was supposed to be resting.

Gavin had a wife and two children that he rarely saw, due to his long working hours. At first, he hid the news from his family, fearing his wife's reaction. They lived in a huge house on a leafy road in a very upmarket area just outside London; his wife was a 'lady-who-lunches' and his kids were at private school. Gavin was afraid that his illness meant he would not be able to afford to work which would mean giving up the lifestyle to which his family had grown accustomed. Therefore, he pretended that everything was ok.

The longer Gavin lied to work and his family, the more uptight he became. However, the doctor had told him that 'stress' would only exacerbate his cancer so not only was he stressed but he was stressed about getting stressed. He was also terrified that the 'stress' would shift his focus from his job, and he wouldn't perform as well as he used to. His biggest fear was losing his job; then he would be unemployed and ill, a situation he refused to let himself get into.

The thing was that Gavin had known for some time that there was something not quite right with his health. He had been experiencing difficulty passing urine, and was going to the toilet more often than usual, especially at night. However, he was afraid to get it checked out in case it was bad news, and he knew he wouldn't be able to deal with the consequences:

> 'I knew there was something wrong with my prostate but I ignored it. I told myself it would go away; the idea of actually having cancer was too much to handle, so I buried my head in the sand, and just got on with it.'

The problem there was that Gavin wasn't 'just getting on with it', he was actually living in fear and uncertainty. If you think about it, in this case, living in uncertainty is actually worse than living with certainty, whatever that certainty may be. At least if you receive a diagnosis you can take steps to address the health problem; otherwise you're just living in fear.

Rome wasn't built in a day

We tend to see a diagnosis as a threat to our integrity. When the doctor tells us we have a serious illness, we tend to see all the threats at once and feel bombarded by a rush of hundreds of thoughts. Gavin's first reaction was that he was going to die, quickly followed by what on earth he was going to do about work, the affect his illness would have on his family, and then the treatment he would have to take etc. These thoughts swirled around his head until he felt totally overwhelmed by the amount of stuff he needed to sort out.

In reality, there is absolutely no rush to sort everything out at once. You are better off addressing everything else after you have given yourself time to assimilate the information. Making decisions when you are calmer is far more effective than running around in a blind panic, scaring yourself and everyone else around you.

In fact, sometimes it can actually be more helpful to be in denial, initially, rather than feeling overwhelmed and panicky. However, this is not a helpful coping mechanism in the long term as the symptoms of your illness still need to be addressed and adjustments made.

Step up to the plate

So, before you go around making calls to everybody you know about your diagnosis, take some time to sit down to really think about it. Firstly, you don't actually need to tell anybody anything. Only tell people when you have fully accepted the diagnosis and are entirely knowledgeable about it. Let's face it, whenever we mention the 'c' word, people think 'death'. It is likely they are going to freak out in the same way you probably did when you first heard the news.

Therefore, if you haven't accepted your diagnosis and are ill-equipped to answer questions about it, the likelihood is you will end up stressing each other out by second-guessing the worst. The person you have told will probably know absolutely nothing about your illness and will be tempted to put in their tuppence-worth, based on rumour or inaccurate facts, for example: 'Well, I heard of a girl who had the exact same illness as you, and she lost a leg' or some such baseless story.

Strange though it may sound, for others to give you the support you want, you need to be in a position to reassure them by telling them all the facts and information about your illness, so that they can do their best to help you. Think about why you are telling that person; how will you, or they, benefit from knowing? What are the ways in which they can help you? The relationship needs to be mutually beneficial to a certain degree but, as the person who is ill, it needs to be even more beneficial for you in order to help with your recovery.

In short, only tell people when you are ready and have enough knowledge about your condition to provide answers to their questions. That way, you are on the right path towards getting the support you need.

Storm the winter palace

So, before you spread the news, do your research and get as many facts as you can about your condition. It has been proven that those who educate themselves with up to date information around their condition cope a whole lot better emotionally. Make out a list of questions and sit down with your doctor. If you are not satisfied with some of the answers, then go out and seek the advice of another professional. Some people find researching their condition on the internet is helpful as it normalizes the illness. For example, Gavin was embarrassed about his prostate cancer, but he was comforted to find that there were thousands of sufferers out there who were experiencing the same problem.

However, there is such a thing as too much information. If we go overboard and do too much research, the information might start to become contradictory. There is a lot of misleading information on the internet and if we believe all of it, we begin to identify with symptoms that we don't actually have. So, don't seek too much information at once.

In your quest for knowledge, also bear in mind that the medical field doesn't know everything. When they do know something it is their job to give you the worst case scenario. Believe it or not, some people actually cope better when they are provided with the most information, unpleasant though it is, as it is a way of preparing them for what might happen. It is vital that you are up to date and well informed about your illness. However, fundamentally, it is up to you to make your own experience.

Role swap

A medical condition doesn't just affect the person who has it; it also has an affect on everybody else, especially those closest to you at home and at work. For example, Gavin was advised to rest for a while at home following treatment for his prostate cancer, and found the whole experience extremely difficult. He had always been the provider, the money-maker, the one who took care of his wife and two kids. Being cared for, rather than being the carer, was a big shock to him.

Illness can skew the relationship between many couples. This is an adjustment process for both parties and it can be difficult to deal with. Gavin found that he wasn't the type of person that wanted to be looked after, but when he tried to do things for himself and failed, he became very frustrated and angry. He started to resent the role swap and had fits of temper which left his wife and children upset and resentful.

Every time his wife would complain about something, which had absolutely nothing to do with his illness, he would snap at her, in a sarcastic manner:

> 'Oh, so the traffic was bad today? Poor you, it must be terrible to have to suffer all that. I have cancer. Look how much I have to deal with! Please have some perspective!'

When we are ill, we often think others do not have the right to moan or complain, because, surely, no matter what their issue is, it can't be as bad as what we're going through, right? This is how insular we can become when a serious illness takes over our lives. Illness means we are possibly feeling under-confident, so some part of us may feel it necessary to second-guess any further threat from our environment so as not to be, unexpectedly, shocked and traumatized by it. Therefore, we may find ourselves quick to interpret our partners' or work colleagues' comments as personal slights or attacks and believe that they are being inconsiderate towards us.

However, just because we view the complaints of others as 'attacking' or trivial doesn't mean we can't take their feelings into consideration. We need to allow for other people's experiences, and avoid comparing each individual situation with our own. Furthermore, it is possible that we misinterpret this 'lack of consideration' from others which is unhelpful to our relationships.

Letting it all out

However, if you do feel quite strongly about other people's 'trivial' moaning then it is better to get it out in the open rather than bottling it all up, and losing your temper with them. For example, using the communication techniques described in Chapter Eight, Gavin explained to his wife:

> Gavin: 'I *feel* quite angry when I hear you complain about trivial things such as the bad traffic, as I tend to think that you don't understand what I am going through.'
>
> His wife: 'I *heard* you say that you feel angry when I make complaints about trivial things as you tend to think that I don't understand what you are going through. Is that right?'
>
> Gavin: 'Yes, that is what I said'.
>
> His wife: 'I *understand* that you would feel angry when I make complaints about trivial things if you were to think that this meant I don't understand what you are going through. I will try to be more aware of this when I do it.'
>
> His wife: 'However, I am not suggesting that the traffic is more important than your illness. I understand that you must be in pain and I feel for you, I really do. It's just sometimes I get frustrated too.'

By using language such as 'I feel', 'I heard' and 'I understand', Gavin feels he is being empathized with and now also understands how is wife is feeling. He realizes that his illness is 'not all about him' and he needs to be there for his wife and family as much as they are there for him.

Similarly, when returning to work, Gavin's colleagues seemed to treat him differently, as he had feared. He was given menial tasks to complete and he felt undervalued and disrespected. Gavin decided to speak to his work colleagues and managers about how he was feeling. He learned that people at work did not want to assume that he was fit to get straight back into his old role, and the allocation of the small amount of work was meant in a supportive way. Therefore, Gavin was able to devise a gradual and structured plan with his manager to increase his working days, and the intensity of his projects, over time. After a while, he started to feel more at ease among his colleagues and felt more confident when they began to look to him for technical guidance one more.

Speaking the same language

Illness can be very isolating and it is extremely important to have support around you. The side-effects of medical treatment can really put you out of action. For example, the side-effects of medication to treat HIV and cancer can be extremely severe, and may require your partner to look after you, wash and feed you etc.

The type of language we use is particularly crucial when one party is feeling much weaker than the other. Emotional support is about listening and providing understanding and empathy; for example, saying: 'It's not that bad' or 'I feel so sorry for you' is not helpful for the ill patient.

Instead, use empathic phrases such as 'I understand that must be difficult for you'. Also, ask lots of open questions: 'What's that like for you?' 'Is there anything I can do to help you?' 'How are you feeling?' These types of enquiries will encourage more of an honest response from the person who is ill, who will feel comforted by your empathy, genuine concern, and curiosity in relation to how they are feeling.

Swallowing the pride

It can be a blow to our pride when we are put into a position where we need to be cared for. The best way to deal with the shift in dynamic is to talk about how you are feeling. By accepting your situation and your new role you are already on the right path towards making the best out of a difficult situation:

> 'Maybe it's ok that I'm being cared for even though I'm usually the one that cares for others. I am still very competent in many ways and the more I accept and remind myself of this, the stronger I might feel and the more I may be able to do it again as a result.'

Then think about all the things you can do rather than what you can't. For example, Gavin acknowledged that he wouldn't be able to carry out some of his usual tasks around the house but still wanted to help out his wife in other ways:

> 'I may not be able to bring the rubbish out for a little while, or bring the kids out at the weekends, but what can I do to help you out?

His wife told him he could give her a hand folding laundry, which they started to do together every morning. During this time, they would chat, sometimes about his cancer, but, more often than not, just about general stuff, like how the kids were doing in school etc. Due to his long working hours, Gavin had very much been, in the past, a 'weekend husband and dad' and rarely had time to spend with his wife, let alone with the kids. After a spell at home, he grudgingly admitted that it was nice to have quality time with his family.

Dealing with death

Admittedly, illnesses like cancer, heart disease, and HIV etc., are potentially life-threatening but medicine is so advanced, these diseases rarely mean death any more. However, when we receive a diagnosis, it is completely natural to think about dying. But if we spend all our time worrying about death, it will certainly worsen our symptoms.

There is nothing wrong about talking about death for any of us; death is a part of life and we all need to accept that. However, obsessing about it and worrying about it will not do any of us any good. The irony of receiving a diagnosis is that you are actually more informed about yourself and your health than hundreds and thousands of other people, who walk around everyday with dangerously high blood pressure or HIV and don't even know it. Without sounding too trite about it, finding out we have a health problem may not be such a bad position to be in. It enables you to address the problem straight away, whereas most people who have no idea about their health might not even get the opportunity to treat their own disease.

You can now move forward and look to the future. Receiving a diagnosis does not have to be that catastrophic; it may be about dramatic life changes, such as doing less hours at work, a shift in the dynamic of your relationships, and taking medical treatment, but it's about an adjustment process: it's not the end; it's simply a new way of being.

Shifting the focus

I had a friend who was diagnosed with heart disease. His condition was quite serious and he was told that he could have a heart attack at any time. When he got the news, he began to repeatedly check his blood pressure and pulse. Sometimes he panicked when he thought he couldn't find a pulse, or felt that it was really weak, which made him even more anxious. The doctor had actually told him that checking his pulse and blood pressure were not indicators of his condition, but he wouldn't accept this and continued to go through his hourly ritual.

If his blood pressure came back normal, he would check it again just in case it wasn't an accurate reading or there was something wrong with the machine he was using. When his heart beat faster, he would think he was in danger. However, he would interpret any 'normal' bodily sensation as catastrophic. He would see every pang of anxiety as a sign he was going to keel over any second. Of course, the more anxious he became about his heart, the more it beat faster. When this happened, he was sure he was having a heart attack.

The grass is always greener ...

My friend also had a fear of exerting himself in case it brought about more heart problems. Because of his condition, he felt like he couldn't do anything or go anywhere. When I asked him what sort of things he felt he was missing out on, he told me:

> 'Well, say I wanted to go for a walk by myself in the country-side. I couldn't do that because I can't go anywhere on my own, in case I have a heart attack. I need people around me to call the ambulance, if necessary.'

Now, bearing in mind that my friend was more of a 'City Slicker' than a country boy, and the least likely person I could think of that would want to venture deep into the countryside (unless it was to a country pub), I asked him why he would want to do that particular activity in the first place. He replied:

> 'It's not like I want to go for a walk in the country; actually, I hate the countryside. It's more to do with the fact that I can't, even if I wanted to. That avenue has been cut off from me.'

The point is that my friend was focusing on all the things he couldn't do, instead of all the things he could do.

In the end, he took up Yoga, Pilates, and started going for brisk walks at lunchtime during work, none of which he had ever done before. He started to really enjoy his new activities. Not only were they good for him, but they proved to be valuable distracting techniques and helped take his mind off his illness. He also started to do some relaxation, meditation, and breathing exercises. He no longer checked his pulse and blood pressure a million times a day, and found himself a lot less anxious then before.

When we are diagnosed with an illness, it is really hard to see the silver lining; in fact, it may sound facetious or flippant to even mention a more optimistic perspective on illness. However, in his case, if he hadn't been diagnosed with this problem, he would never have engaged in any of these enjoyable activities. They may only have been small lifestyle changes but, already, they had improved his perspective of his condition, and helped to get him a bit more fit, into the bargain!

Dealing with the kids

It is hard enough to admit you are ill to your partner, let alone the kids, but it is important that they know what is going on. Again, honest and factual communication comes into play here. Hiding it will only bring about more problems; for example, if you suddenly stop doing all the things you did before with your children, like taking them to after school activities or weekend outings, then they might think you don't want to spend time with them anymore.

However, only tell them about your condition when you are completely confident about it yourself. Most children are curious creatures and they will be sure to have lots of questions. Depending on the age of the child, and the seriousness of your condition, it is ok to talk about death as long as it is discussed in an open and honest way.

At first, Gavin had a hard time saying no to his youngest son when he wanted to kick the footie around in the back garden—an early morning ritual. His six year old simply couldn't understand why his dad wouldn't play with him. Gavin would end up snapping at him, and his little boy would run off angry or in tears. Eventually, Gavin sat him down and explained about his illness and what that meant for the family, and together, they reached an agreement about the footie:

> 'Daddy might not be able to play football with you for the moment, but maybe we can do something else together, like watch a football DVD instead.'

By suggesting another activity to replace the previous one, Gavin and his son were still able to spend time together.

Strike while the iron is hot

As you can see, Gavin had a habit of procrastinating. He didn't know how to tell his family or his work colleagues about his illness; and as a result he hid it from them which caused him more anxiety.

Procrastination is a waste of time. It is a very common and often the most significant maintaining factor of our psychological distress. In not getting on with tasks we do not provide ourselves with the opportunity to show ourselves what we *can* do. Procrastination leaves us feeling helpless and stuck; it goes against our innate tendency to strive forward and be productive in life. We lose confidence in ourselves as we tend to beat ourselves up about all that we're not getting done. Most of us will put uninspiring tasks to the back of the queue but if we do this too often, they have a habit of building up and overwhelming us. When we are afraid of something, like illness, or an intimidating work project, it is easier to avoid dealing with it than accepting it.

Dos and Don'ts for procrastination

- *Don't* wait until you are 'in the mood' to tackle a problem. Some situations can be so boring or unpleasant that the chances are you will never be in the right frame of mind to deal with them. So, get on with it and reward yourself when you get the task done.
- *Do* make a list of reasons why you are putting off the task. This is particularly useful when it comes to a work project that you simply don't feel like doing. Listing the advantages and disadvantages of delaying the project will help you figure out what is stopping you from progressing with it.

- *Don't* look at the task as one giant effort. Break it up into manageable pieces and set deadlines for the completion of each step.
- *Do* set timelines in advance for each part of the task. For example: 'I will spend 30 minutes making calls about the project' or 'I will spend 10 minutes organising meetings to talk about the project.'
- *Don't* beat yourself up about not doing the task and watch your language! Try and replace the guilty 'I should', or 'I have to' with 'I would prefer to' or 'I choose to'.
- *Do* make time to plan the task and put it on your 'To Do' list. Complete the most unpleasant task at the beginning of the day so it isn't hanging over you for the rest of the time.
- *Don't* sit there and worry continually about it; remember: it is worse to live in uncertainty than certainty, so dive in and get started. You will probably find that once you get stuck in, the task isn't as bad as you first thought.
- *Do* review your 'To Do' list at the end of each month to assess your progression with the task. Did you meet your deadlines? Did it turn out as well as you expected? If not, then make sure you learn from your mistakes so you can apply them to the next project.

The upshot

Gavin recovered well from his prostate cancer and made a gradual return to work. He learned to welcome the support from his work colleagues and was honest and open about what he needed from them. At home, he found his illness had, in a weird way, brought him closer to his family, and he really looked forward to, and valued, the time they spent together.

Dealing with a serious diagnosis is extremely difficult, and it can be almost impossible to see the silver lining. However, it is all about trying to focus on alternatives, and finding different ways of being that may not actually be that unbearable after all. It's not that being ill isn't a problem; of course it's a problem, but maybe just one we have to deal with, like any other.

Being ill is a knock to our confidence and self-worth, and because of this, it is important to focus on what we do have, the things in life we can be certain about such as the support of friends and family; the medication that will help; and support from work colleagues etc.

You might not think there is any benefit to being ill, but if you approach your illness in the right way; arm yourself with the necessary information; use the right communication skills; and make the most of the support of those closest to you; you may realize that your diagnosis does not mean it's the end of your world, but, perhaps, just the beginning of a new chapter in your life.

A FINAL WORD

As I write this, the country is in recession, the level of unemployment has risen to over two million, and the City is being hit hard by the collapse of some major financial institutions. Things could be better.

However, I hope some of the techniques and exercises I have suggested in this book do help you to overcome your worries and problems, and view things from a different, and more helpful perspective. Redundancy and unemployment are all very difficult situations to deal with but it is important that you are aware that it is not the end of the world if you lose your job, but how you deal with it that counts.

The thought of job insecurity and redundancy activates our innate insecurities. It is understandable that we will worry about our future stability or ruminate about what we have lost. It is important, however, to remember that we cannot control that which is outside of us, but we can learn ways to manage ourselves in the face of stressful life events. By focusing on what we cannot control we start to feel more stuck, under confident, and helpless which increases the likelihood of becoming depressed or anxious. No matter how distressing our current situation may be, it will inevitably change and with change always comes new possibilities.

The exercises and methods in this book are certainly simple, fast, and easy to use. However, they do need a certain amount of commitment in order to work, so do make an effort to practice these techniques until they become second nature to you. It may take a little while but the important thing is not to give up. So make sure your lists, tables and diaries are close to hand and review them on a regular basis. This will help you to monitor your progress and will give you faith if you slip up. The more you practice the higher your confidence, self-esteem, and self-worth will be. You will find yourself worrying less, and making time for the important things in life, more.

Similarly, providing support to a friend or relative who may be experiencing some of these problems is not easy either; however, if you listen to them and support them in a helpful way, it can make a real difference to their progress.

And more importantly, remember that the route to *staying sane in the square mile* is all about self-awareness and self-acceptance. So, try and not let the doom and gloom get you down, and make a commitment to yourself to tackle your problems in the most beneficial way possible.

Breathing

"For breath is life, and if you breathe well you will live long on earth."
Sanskrit Proverb

Most of us take breathing for granted; after all, it's something we do all the time and it is understandable that we may not be conscious of it. However, poor breathing habits can restrict the flow of oxygen into our bodies and the release of carbon dioxide out of our bodies. This can result in increased anxiety, panic attacks, muscle tension, exhaustion, irritability, and physical symptoms such as headaches.

Being aware of your breathing and practising the way you breathe will help to calm your mind and relax your body. Breathing exercises can be useful if they are practised on their own, but they are especially helpful when practised with other relaxation exercises such as meditation (please see Appendix II for an example of a meditation exercise).

Overbreathing

In several of the chapters, we have explored the topic of anxiety and how it can manifest itself in many ways, including panic attacks.

Hyperventilation or overbreathing is very common during panic attacks. When we begin to overbreathe, we tend to breathe faster and/or deeper than we need to. This means we take in more oxygen then necessary which can result in the following symptoms:

- Light headedness
- Dizziness
- Shortness of breath
- Sweating
- Heart palpitations
- Chest pains
- Tingling/numbness
- Clammy hands
- Difficulty swallowing
- Blurred vision
- Weakness
- Fatigue

Contrary to popular belief, hyperventilation is not a result of too little oxygen, but too little carbon dioxide. Breathing in too much air at a rapid pace reduces the carbon dioxide in our blood which causes the above symptoms. Thus, in order to correct the balance between oxygen and carbon dioxide we must learn to control and master our breathing.

Spotting the signs

If you are susceptible to panic attacks, then you will come to know the initial signs. You may feel tightness in your chest; a feeling of being trapped; or you are breathing too fast. When this happens:

- Down tools, leave your desk (or whatever task you are doing) and seek out a quiet place. If you are at work, then try and find a free meeting room, where you can close the door, leaving yourself free from any interruptions.
- Sit down and close your eyes. Focus on a soothing phrase or word (the same way as explained in the Meditation exercise in Appendix II) such as 'calm' or 'peace'.
- Try some mini PMR exercises (Appendix III) such as hunching your shoulders, and letting them drop and relax. A tense upper

body only increases the level of overbreathing so try and relax that part of your body as far as possible.

- Breathe very slowly: in through your nose, and out through your mouth. Take a deep breath in to a count of four and exhale to a count of four. If you do this properly, you should be taking about 10 to 12 breaths per minute.

You may find that, after a few minutes, you are still feeling anxious and panicky. In this situation, you may need to try breathing in your own carbon dioxide to address the balance in your lungs. Some people find breathing in and out of a brown paper bag useful. However, if there is not one to hand, then simply:

- Cup your hands and place them over your nose and mouth, as in the below diagram.

Figure 11. Technique to overcome hyperventilation.

- Breathe in through your nose and breathe out hard through your mouth.
- Breathe slowly and smoothly. Repeat four or five times.
- Try and think calm and relaxing thoughts. Thinking about how anxious and breathless we are will only exacerbate the situation.
- Remember: your symptoms may be unpleasant and scary but you won't stop breathing or die! Try and stay as calm as possible while telling yourself that the symptoms will pass soon enough.

Monitoring your breathing

The best way to master your breathing is to become conscious of it. You may find that your breathing is too shallow or that you tend to breathe through your mouth rather than through your nose. Yawning excessively is also another indication of improper breathing habits. In order to become more aware of your breathing, try the following exercise:

- Lie down and close your eyes.
- Put one hand on your abdomen/diaphragm and the other on the centre of your chest.
- Breathe as you would normally.

Figure 12. Monitor your breathing.

You may find that your abdomen moves less than your chest. If this is the case then you will know that you are breathing more from your chest than your abdomen. This means that you will need to change your breathing so you breathe from your abdomen rather than your chest.

- Lie down and place both your hands on your abdomen.
- Breathe in slowly through your nose and feel your abdomen rise under your hands.
- As you exhale, your abdomen will fall.

Once you have mastered the art of breathing correctly, you will find that your mind is clearer, and your mental and physical symptoms much improved.

Meditation

"What's encouraging about meditation is that even if we shut down, we can no longer shut down in ignorance. We see very clearly that we're closing off. That in itself begins to illuminate the darkness of ignorance."

—Perma Chodron

Meditation is great for relaxing your mind and putting you into a calmer state. If your mind is settled, your body will follow. Thus, frequent meditation will help to relieve the anxiety of our busy lives. Many people attend meditation classes; however, you can also practise meditation at home. The more you practise, the easier it becomes and you will reach a point where you will know exactly what you need to do to quickly put your mind and body into a relaxed state.

There is no set time for meditation, but even 10 minutes a day can make a difference. So, have a look at the following simple exercise and give it a try!

- Find a quiet place where you will not be distracted or disturbed. Dim the lights, if possible.
- Make sure you are sitting or lying comfortably.

- Close your eyes.
- Begin by breathing deeply through your nose and out through your mouth. Think about the cool air as it comes in through your nose, and how warm and moist it feels when you exhale through your mouth. Continue breathing in this way until you feel completely relaxed.
- Pick a word or phrase that you feel is soothing, lie 'calm', or 'peace' and repeat the word to yourself every time you breathe out.
- Try some visualisation techniques to help you 'mentally switch off'. Think of a place, real or imaginary, where you can really relax. This could be walking along a beach or sailing on calm waters.
- Think about what you can see or hear in this place; the sounds of the waves lapping on the shore; the whiteness of the sand; and the smell of the sea air. Imagine touching the sand or trailing your hand through the cool water, and just let yourself drift away ...
- Thoughts or worries may intrude on your meditation, acknowledge them and accept they are just thoughts and let them pass. Concentrate on your breathing and repeating your calming word/phrase.
- When you feel ready, open your eyes and count backwards from 10. When you reach 1, rise slowly and give yourself time to adjust before getting on with your day.

Meditation can be practised at any time of the day, but it can be particularly effective in the morning before you go to work, in order to clear and prepare your mind for the day ahead; and in the evening, in order to relax your mind after a busy day at the office.

Relaxation

"Tension is who you think you should be. Relaxation is who you are."
Chinese Proverb

Relaxation exercises can really help to improve our body and mind by removing the physical/mental tension we feel as a result of our busy lives. Of course, there are many ways to relax: some people take a walk, listen to music, or take a bath. However, others find it difficult to relax at all, even after these activities, and need to learn specific techniques to help them recover from everyday stresses and strains.

Taking Yoga or Meditation classes (see Appendix II for some meditation exercises) is a very useful way to learn more about relaxation. But if you don't have time to take these classes then have a look at the below simple exercises which will really help to take the tension out of your day.

Frankie says …

When we lead such fast-paced lives it seems impossible to think we have the time to relax at all. However, here are some reasons why relaxation is helpful:

- When we worry our whole body can feel unpleasantly tense, which brings about a range of physical symptoms, including: shoulder pain, back pain, chest pain etc.
- Physical aches and pains cause us to worry even more about our own health, for example, a feeling of tightness in the chest may be interpreted as the onset of a heart attack. The more we worry, the worse the feeling will get.
- Relaxation exercises help to relieve the physical aches and pains and remove the tension in our mind and body, leaving us feeling calmer, less tired, and more confident in our ability to cope with the day ahead.

Tips for relaxation preparation

- Make a note to yourself deciding when and where you are going to take time out to relax, and stick to it!
- Find a quiet place and make sure there is nobody around to disturb you.
- Make sure you are ready to relax, for example, don't try these exercises if are starving as all you will be thinking about is food! Ensure that your body is comfortable and you are open to trying out the exercises.
- Breathe properly! (Have a look at Appendix I for some Breathing Exercises). Breathing is fundamental to our well-being and is of vital importance when trying to relax.

Relaxation in work

- Take lots of breaks; there is absolutely no merit to sitting in front of your computer all day; this will only cause muscle tension in your back and shoulders (especially if you are not sitting properly) and will leave you mentally and physically exhausted.
- Reward yourself when you achieve a goal in work such as taking a walk to the shops, or arranging to have a coffee with a friend;

anything that will get you away from your desk for more than five minutes. You have worked hard for your treat, so you deserve it!

• Book yourself in for a massage during the week if you can. It's something to look forward to and will help you feel more relaxed for a few days afterwards.

Relaxing our body

Progressive Muscular Relaxation (PMR) is an excellent exercise for relaxing the tension in the muscles all over our body. It also helps to figure out which of those muscles are causing the most tension, allowing us to focus on those areas a little longer than others.

• Set aside 15 minutes for this exercise. You may wish to practise it twice a day until you get the hang of it.
• Sit or lie down comfortably in a quiet place and take a few deep breaths.
• Tense and hold each set of muscular exercises (as outlined below) for about 5 seconds. Then relax for 10 to 15 seconds before moving on to the next muscle group. Think about the tension flowing out of the muscles and how they feel when you tense them. Repeat each exercise until you feel relaxed but don't push yourself too hard.

PMR exercise

Figure 13. Progressive muscular relaxation exercise.

- Raise your eyebrows as high as possible. Hold for a few seconds and then relax them, noticing the tension flowing away.
- Squeeze your eyes shut tightly and hold them there. Relax your eyes, still keeping them closed as you notice the tension fading away.
- Clench your jaw by pressing your back teeth together. Gradually relax your jaw.
- Scrunch up your whole face: nose, eyes and mouth. Relax as the tension flows away from you face.
- Push your chin slowly against your chest. Allow the muscles in your neck and shoulders to tense. Relax as you slowly lift your chin again.
- Stretch out your arms and clench your fists and hold for a few seconds. Slowly relax your arms again as you open your fists and notice the tension flowing out from your fingers and forearms.
- Hunch your shoulders and then let them relax slowly.
- Clench the muscles in your stomach as tight as you can, then gradually relax.
- Stretch out your legs and point your toes upwards. Feel the tension in your thigh and calf muscles. Hold for a few seconds and then relax.
- Tense your whole body. Hold for a few seconds and relax. Check and see if there are still any areas that feel tense. If so, then repeat the tensing and relaxing exercises until they also feel relaxed.
- Take a few deep breaths and, when you are ready, open your eyes. Briefly stretch your arms and legs and get up slowly when you feel you are ready to face the day again.

Like everything, relaxation exercises take commitment and practise. However, once you master them, you will find that they really help to reduce your levels of anxiety and remove tension from your mind and body.

USEFUL CONTACTS

Alcohol Concern
Waterbridge House
32–36 Loman Street
London, SE1 0EE
Tel: 020 7 9287377

Beat (beating eating disorders)
103 Prince of Wales Road
Norwich
NR1 1DW
United Kingdom
Tel: 0845 634 1414
Fax: 0160 366 4915
Email: help@b-eat.co.uk
Website: www.b-eat.co.uk

British Association for Behavioural and Cognitive Psychotherapies
P.O. Box 9
Accrington, BB5 0RE
Tel: 01254 875 277
Fax: 01254 239 114
Email: babcp@babcp.com
Website: www.babcp.com

British Association for Counselling and Psychotherapy
1 Regent Place
Rugby
Warwickshire, CV21 2PJ
Tel: 0788 578 328
www.counselling.co.uk

British Pain Society
The Secretariat
The Pain Society
21 Portland Place
London, W1B 1PY
Tel: 020 7631 8870
Website: www.britishpainsociety.org

British Psychological Society (BPS)
St Andrews House
48 Princess Road East
Leicester LE1 7DR
Tel: 0116 254 9568
Fax: 0116 247 0787
Email: enquiry@bps.org.uk
Website: www.bps.org.uk

City Psychology Group
1st Floor
55 Old Broad Street
London, EC2M 1RX
Tel: 0845 01 77 838
Fax: 020 8711 5444
Email: contact@city-psychology.co.uk
Website: www.city-psychology.co.uk

CRUSE Bereavement Care
Cruse House
126 Sheen Road
Richmond
Surrey, TW9 1UR
Tel: 020 89404818
Website: www.crusebereavementcare.org.uk

Depersonalisation Research Unit
Section of Cognitive Neuropsychiatry, PO68
Division of Psychological Medicine and Psychiatry
Institute of Psychiatry
De Crespigny Park
London, SE5 8AF
Tel: 020 7848 0138
Fax: 020 7848 0572
Website: www.iop.kcl.ac.uk

DrugScope
Waterbridge House
32–36 Loman Street
London, SE1 0EE
Tel: 020 7928 1211
Website: www.drugscope.org.uk

Macmillan Cancer Support
89 Albert Embankment
London, SE1 7UQ
Tel: 020 7840 7840
Fax: 020 7840 7841
Website: www.macmillan.org.uk

Mind
Granta House
15–19 Broadway
Stratford
London, E15 4BQ
Tel: 020 8519 2122
Website: www.mind.org.uk

PACE (promoting lesbian and gay health and wellbeing)
34 Hartham Road
London
N7 9LJ
Tel: 020 7700 1323
Fax: 020 7609 4909
Email: info@pace.dircon.co.uk
Website: www.pacehealth.org.uk

Parentline Plus
520 Highgate Studios
53–79 Highgate Road
Kentish Town
London, NW5 1TL
Tel: 020 7284 5500
Website: www.parentlineplus/org.uk

Phobic Action
Greater London House
547–551 High Road
London, E11 4PB
Tel: 020 8558 3463

Prostate Cancer Charity
First Floor
Cambridge House
100 Cambridge Grove
Hammersmith
London, W6 0LE.
Tel: 020 8222 7622
Fax: 020 8222 7639
Email: info@prostate-cancer.org.uk
Website: www.prostatecancer.org.uk

Relate
Herbert Gray College
Little Church Street
Rugby
Warwickshire, CV21 3AP
Tel: 0870 601 2121
Website: www.relate.org.uk

SAD Association
P.O. Box 989
Steyning
West Sussex, BN44 3HG
Tel: 01903 814942
Website: www.sada.org.uk

Samaritans
P.O. Box 9090
Stirling
FK8 2SA
Tel: 0845 790 9090
Fax: 0160 366 4915
Email: jo@samaritans.org
Website: www.samaritans.org

Terrence Higgins Trust
Lighthouse Kings
Unit 2 Empress Mews
Kenbury St
Camberwell
London
SE5 9BT
Tel: 020 7737 9740
Fax: 020 7737 9741
Email: info.camberwell@tht.org.uk
Website: www.tht.org.uk

UKCP (United Kingdom Council for Psychotherapy)
167 Great Portland Street
London, W1N 5FB
Tel: 020 7436 3002
www.psychotherapy.org.uk

INDEX